The Sears Wish Book

I was six years old and all I wanted for Christmas was a vanity. It had Barbie decals on it. It was built for little girls my age. It was pink and white plastic with little spindly legs. It had a wavy not quite glass mirror. It had little drawers with compartments for plastic pretend compact makeup and lipsticks. It also came with a little plastic stool. It was glorious in it's uselessness.

I found this in the Sears Wish Book and I couldn't take my eyes off of it. I wrote to Santa and there was only one thing on my list. I told Santa that I hoped he had liked the cookies the year before. I was kind of buttering him up. I got the impression from my mother that Santa was not a big fan of these Barbie Vanities.

Ma told me that even the elves admitted the workmanship on this vanity was a little shoddy. She added that any one leaning on that thing would just snap the legs off. She had heard that little girls with only that on their lists should really sit down and come up with another list.

She tried to hand the Sears catalog to me again. I wouldn't take it. She flipped to the doll section. She pointed out burping dolls. Dolls that couldn't keep a diaper dry. Dolls with hair that grew.

I just shook my head no at her. Santa was the smartest guy around. If he thought the vanity wasn't strong enough he would surely get involved and improve it. There had to be some standards up at the North Pole. Some quality control. This is Santa we're talking about! I was not making another list.

I knew what I wanted and that was it. The end.

One day my mother was busy making spaghetti and I went down to the basement to investigate. My father had been down there all day and my mother had been guarding the basement door like a bull dog.

I could hear his circular saw. I could hear the banging of his hammer. I was usually his helper girl. I was always allowed to help. How could he possibly get anything done without me down there to hand him nails one at a time from the bag.

So, I just sneaked by my mother. I walked down the stairs and stood looking at him at his work bench. I saw that he was building a low flat box out of spare paneling. It had a shiny pink formica top. He was fitting a drawer into the middle when I arrived.

He glanced down at me and froze. He lay down his tools and tried to turn me around.

"I smell spaghetti, Little Girl. I think Mommy sure could use some help setting the table." he said.

"Nope!" I replied. "Table is all set! I picked out five forks, five spoons and five knives Daddy. I even put napkins next to the plates." I beamed at him.

"Whatcha making?" I asked. "And how can you nail things without me? That's my job!." I declared.

He swept a half a bag full of paneling nails into the drawer. He said "Sorry, Little Girl, all done nailing today. No more nailing. You go upstairs now. Help your mother………. Ellie! Darlene wants to help you" he yelled in the direction of the stairs.

My mother couldn't come to his rescue at that moment. She told me later that she was draining the pasta and couldn't step away.

I stepped forward and ran my hand over the low long box. "What is this Daddy? What are you making?"

"Um………..well, I am…….you see……………um……….what is this? It's a bird house. Yes, a bird house! I'm making a bird house for Grammy's yard. She loves her blue birds." he explained.

"That's a really big bird house!" I said. I'd seen the ones he had built with my brother. They were small little things that you hung in the branches of the apple tree. I told him this.

"Well! This here is a very special bird house because it's a Christmas present. This is a Bird Apartment Complex. " he explained.

"Oh!" I said. "Grammy will like that! Lots of birds all in one place. Can I help with the brush and varnish when it's time to make it shiny? You hardly ever let me help with that part." I put out my bottom lip. He fell for that one every time.

"We'll see, Little Girl. We'll see." he said as he looked up at my mother. She had come to rescue him.

"Time for dinner." she said. "Let's march, Little Girl."

Christmas Eve came and we drove over to my grandparent's house just as it was getting dark. I never could stay awake in that car if it was getting dark. When we pulled into their driveway in Glastonbury I awoke and was excited to see their little Christmas tree all lit up in the livingroom window.

My grandparents were Swedish. They put lights on their tree but they decorated it with little wrapped gifts for all of us. My parents put their gifts for them under the tree.

We had raspberry cookies and other treats. I even got a taste of coffee with lots of milk in it.

We opened presents. One of my little packages held handmade mittens. Another was a beautiful purple hat with white angora tassels. My favorite of all was a little plastic nativity that sat in the palm of my hand. I would still own that as a grownup.

My grandparents opened their gifts. They were very happy with the pajamas and robes they got. Then it occurred to me that my Daddy had forgotten to bring the Bird Apartment Complex.

I took his hand and dragged him into the hallway.

"What's the matter, Little Girl? Do you need help in the bathroom? " my father asked. "Don't be afraid of the radiator in there. That hissing noise is just hot water inside of it."

"No, Daddy! I don't have to go to the bathroom. Oh, my goodness, Daddy! You completely forgot to bring the Bird Apartment Complex for Grammy. What are you going to do? It's too far to go back and get it tonight! What are we going to do?" I whispered to him in the hallway.

This was a fiasco!

"Shhhhh! Little Girl. Don't you worry about a thing. We will give it to Grammy for New Years. How about that?

We can keep it a secret until New Years. She will be so happy to hang that bird house and have the birds in her big tree out back. I'm not quite done with it you know. You're going to have to be a helper girl and hand me the nails. How does that sound?" he said. "It'll be our secret."

He calmed me down and brought me back into the livingroom.

I glowed at everyone around the tree because my Daddy and I had a secret!

Christmas morning came bright and early. My brothers jumped around my bed to wake me up. We all ran down to the livingroom to see what Santa had brought us. We banged open our parent's bedroom door. They groaned at us.

I looked around the room but I didn't see anything made out of pink and white plastic. Instead I found a beautiful hand built vanity shining with lustrous varnish. It had a real glass mirror with white flowers etched around the edge. It had a bright shiny yellow top. A little stool with a cushion stood in front of it. I pulled open the drawer and inside were various sweet smelling children's pretend makeup.

I sat down on the stool and looked at myself in the mirror. I saw Daddy's reflection in the mirror behind me. He looked a little nervous.

"What do you think, Little Girl? I think the elves came up with a pretty nice vanity table. It doesn't have Barbie stickers but I think they thought that would ruin the finish." he said to me in the mirror.

"I think this is the most beautiful vanity ever! Daddy! Look! The top is yellow! I think that's even prettier than pink. I love it! Santa is the kindest man that ever lived!" I said as I jumped around the vanity table.

My brothers just rolled their eyes at me.

All the next week I could hear sawing and other noises coming from my father's other work bench in the garage. He usually only worked there on car parts. I wondered what he was doing.

I tried to drag a kitchen chair to the sink to look out. My mother stopped me and put the chair back under the table.

"What is Daddy building out there?" I asked. "It's cold out there. Why doesn't he work downstairs where it is warm next to the furnace?" I wanted to know.

My mother ignored my questions and put a Santa coloring book in front of me.

"Color Daddy a picture right now. He will love that. When he comes in we'll have some nice beef stew and you can give him a picture. I bet he'll put it on the refrigerator. Or, if it's really good he'll take it to work and show all his friends." my mother said as she placed me in a chair.

A few days later Daddy called me down to the basement. Somewhere along the line he had moved his project out of the cold garage.

He had saved a few nails for me. The Bird Apartment Complex still had a pink formica top. But, it somehow looked a little narrower and not quite as long as I remembered it. I noticed there was no opening for a drawer.

I pointed this out to my father and he told me that he had modified it. After thinking about it he thought lots of round holes along the front and the sides were a better choice. Attached to the top of the long box were chains that would be attached to branches.

On New Years Day we arrived at my grandparent's house. We all went inside while my father dragged a ladder out of the garage. He stood on top of the ladder and attached the chains to the middle branches of the tree trying to keep the low, long Bird Apartment Complex level.

My grandparents watched him out of the dining room window. They glanced at each other with questions in their eyes and spoke to each other in Swedish. I can only imagine what they said, but I suppose it was "What the heck is that? That is the biggest bird house I've ever seen! Do you think Ralph is losing it?"

I kept that vanity table for most of my life. It became my desk as a teenager. It sat in the corner of my kitchen when I got married. I put the canister set my mother bought as a shower gift on it. It stood up well. It was still beautiful. It's varnish still shown. The yellow formica matched that first kitchen.

Dad had been caught doing elves work by his little girl that wasn't ready to give up on Santa. He had tried to make my dreams come true and he did. On top of that he continued on to build a bird house his mother would roll her eyes at. Because, that is what he told me he was doing.

My Daddy never lied to me.

****

Catching Santa

It was Christmas Eve. Little Girl had a devious plan. No other little girl had ever thought of doing this!

She had fallen asleep in the car on the way to her grandparent's house. She had fallen asleep on the way home too. It was just impossible to stay awake in that station wagon after darkness fell. No matter what day of the year it was.

Mommy and Daddy had put her to bed. She had a little youth bed in the corner of their bedroom. Her brothers were tucked up in their bunk beds in the other little bedroom on Columbus Street.

Little Girl stretched out in the bed. She stared at shadows on the white ceiling. She was wide awake. The same thing happened to her every time she tried to watch Lassie on TV. Her eyes would close and she'd get carried to bed. The minute her head hit the pillow? She became wide awake. She would lie there wondering if Lassie would ever make it out of that well. Would Lassie ever see Timmy again?

Little Girl listened to the voices of her parents drift through the bedroom door. The kitchen wasn't that far away but they were speaking quietly. She couldn't make out words. She heard the whistle of the tea kettle and cookie cans being opened.

Mommy and Daddy were busy having a tea party on Christmas Eve.

It was time to activate her plan. She slipped from the bed and tiptoed around the corner into the living room. She drank in the sight of the Christmas tree blinking in the corner. The empty stockings hung from the mantlepiece.

Little Girl grabbed a few picture books. If you're in for a long night of waiting? You need something good to read.

She ducked behind the large armchair in the corner of the living room. It was where she usually hid to do her reading when she was supposed to be doing other things. Like folding towels.

It was her hideout. Mommy and Daddy had never figured out her secret spot as far as she knew.

She would catch Santa in the act this year for sure!

Little Girl put her feet up on the white corner wall. She stuffed her teddy bear behind her head and she read for a good half an hour. She was still wide awake. She thought about Christmas mornings.

Santa always worked his magic while they slept. The little living room was neat and clean one minute……………and then overflowing with presents a few hours later. Little Girl was usually the first one up. She'd drag a brother out of bed. She'd hop around the room in excitement proclaiming "Santa is the nicest man in the whole wide world!" at the top of her lungs.

Little Girl's brother was quite a bit older than she was. He would reply "Daddy is a pretty great guy too!" as he started to look for his name on gift tags.

This statement gave Little Girl pause. Well, of course Daddy is a pretty great guy. But, what has that got to do with anything? She wondered about her brother. Maybe he hadn't gotten enough sleep.

She knew Santa was magic. She knew he was a Saint. But, really! The sneakiness of the man was almost creepy! How did he do it? And, all that milk and cookies? In every house! How could one person possibly consume that much without being sick?

You just have to hide out behind a chair and wait for Santa once in a great while. You just have to see it for yourself after too many years of wondering thought Little Girl.

She finished her books. Her mother and father were still talking away in the kitchen. Santa still hadn't come. Little Girl's hand sneaked out from behind the big brown chair. She snagged all the figurines out of the manger scene to play with.

The cow was telling the donkey a story about the first Christmas. There was a big star hanging up in the sky. The angels were helping the shepherds find their sheep. The wise men were wandering around lost. They stopped and asked the innkeeper for directions.

Little Girl yawned a huge yawn and fell asleep on the rug in the corner of the living room.

She woke up when the big chair was being pulled away from the wall.

She heard her Mommy say "Oh, thank God! Put her to bed will you? What will this girl get up to next?" And, then Mommy went down the hallway to bed. Mommy seemed a little cranky.

Daddy picked up Little Girl and put her on his lap. He put his chin into her hair and he breathed in deeply. Then he started to chuckle.

"What on earth are you doing in here, Little Girl? I tucked you into bed myself. And, now I find you on the floor with pieces of the manger all around you. What have you been up to?" he wondered.

"I was waiting for Santa." Little Girl explained. She thought it was pretty obvious. She was about to ask Daddy to wait up with her when she noticed the change.

The stockings bulged. The living room rug had disappeared under all the brightly packaged gifts.

Her eyes flew open wide at the sight of the red and white doll carriage in the corner of the room.

How on earth had she missed Santa? Yet again!

Mommy and Daddy weren't any better at catching Santa than she was! Santa had laid a finger aside of his nose…………and sneaked in while they were busy eating cookies and drinking tea!

Little Girl had never stood a chance.

"How about we put the manger back together. And, then bed. I really really mean it this time, Little Girl." Daddy said.

She put the angels back where they belonged. Mary and Joseph went front and center. Baby Jesus waved his hands in his crib. Little Girl put back the animals last. She put the donkey right next to Mary.

Daddy was always teaching lessons even when he didn't seem to be.

"So, which is the most important figure in this nativity scene, Little Girl?" he asked.

Oh, she knew she should say "The baby Jesus." It was his birthday after all.

"The donkey." Little Girl said as she inched him even closer to Mary.

"The donkey?" Daddy asked in surprise.

"Well, sure! Joseph can't be bothered to pay his taxes on time. So, poor Mary. She's so huge she can hardly waddle. Joseph expects her to walk all that way? He doesn't even make reservations ahead of time at the hotel? It's all about the donkey, Daddy! That donkey said I will give you a ride! Climb on board and let me do the walking! Hang on to my neck and shut your eyes. Have a little nap. I'll get you there...................without this donkey? Christmas would be very different." Little Girl finished.

Daddy looked at his little girl with wonder as he bit into one of the cookies that Santa had left behind. He ignored the warm milk.

"I'm thinking you're going to be quite the storyteller some day, Little Girl! Now, bed!" he said as he lifted her into the air.

Christmas morning came. Little Girl came awake when she heard her brothers whooping in the living room. Her parents groaned when they looked at their clock. The little girl threw back her covers and ran into the living room.

A brother pushed the new doll carriage towards Little Girl. He said "I guess Santa Claus is still the nicest man in the whole wide world." to his little sister with a smile.

Little Girl thought about it. She thought about the elusive Santa. She knew she had given it her best shot the night before. She thought about Daddy carrying her to bed every night when she couldn't keep her eyes open any longer.

"The nicest man in the world?" she asked.

"That would be our Daddy."

****

Barbies and Babies

Barbies. All little girls had them in the 60's. We added to our collections every year under the Christmas tree.

Barbies were for dressing. Barbies didn't hang out in jeans and tee shirts. They wore haute couture. Barbies weren't for hugging and kissing and swaddling in receiving blankets. They were fashion queens.

My mother would sit at the kitchen table and play Barbies with me quite often. Her favorite Barbie dress was a beautiful ball gown. It was irredescent blue and green with a tight bodice and a flowing skirt. Barbie looked like a beautiful humming bird in that dress.

My favorite was a Harlequin Halloween outfit for Skipper. It was black and yellow. It even had a little face mask. She could go to the Halloween Ball and no one would know who she was while wearing that mask.

Mom and I also made Barbie outfits. Mom would save orphan socks and we would cut them up to dress Barbie. Her sewing box had bits and pieces of ribbon and lace and shiny little buttons. We would entertain ourselves for hours while the beef stew was on simmer.

I'm sure the outfits we made weren't beautiful. But, we made them together and Barbie and family seemed happy to be wearing them. My mother taught me the basics of sewing while making Barbie clothing. I learned how to thread a needle. I learned how to make a knot at the end of the thread. I learned basic stitches while I covered Barbies nakedness.

Barbies were for dressing. Any person that has ever dressed a Barbie knows how difficult it can be. Her measurements were non human. Her bust size as compared to her waist size made it difficult to get a dress onto her. There was a lot of pulling and tugging going on. That was a lesson in itself. Barbie was kind of a freak. Real people aren't shaped like this. Way back in the 60's my mother pointed this out to me. She was revolutionary!

Barbies were fun. I loved playing with my mother. But, baby dolls were made for loving.

I loved to love my baby dolls. I would care for my baby dolls. They slept beside me. They were kept warm and fed. They were never left on their own. I cooed to them and rocked them and told them stories.

My mom would say to my father; "Some day she's going to be a good little mother."

One Sunday the family jumped into the station wagon and went to a church picnic. It was not our church. It was my grandparent's church out in Glastonbury. We were Catholic and we were going to a Protestant Church picnic. I wondered if the potato salad would be different.

I brought my baby doll as she couldn't be left unattended at home. She had her own diaper bag full of paraphernalia. It was a really fun afternoon. Protestants turned out to be nice people after all. They even made good potato salad. We were half way home when I realized I had forgotten my baby doll on the picnic bench. I cried in the back seat of the station wagon.

My father didn't want to turn back. He said to my mother "I'll call my parents. Someone at the church must have picked her doll up, Ellie. We can pick it up next week or the next."

My mother turned and looked at me in the back seat. I was squirming around as I was so upset at leaving my baby unattended.

"No, Ralph. Turn around right now. She has to have her baby doll. She can't be without her baby. It's just not right." my mother convinced him.

Christmas came around and I lay down in the living room in front of the fireplace. I flipped the pages of the Sears catalog until I came to the doll section. A beautiful baby carriage caught my eye. It was shining red with white curliques on the side. It had bright white tires and a silver handle. It looked like you could take two babies for a ride in this model. I marked it down on my list. I pictured myself proudly rolling my babies up and down Columbus Street.

Note: It is always best if you give Santa the exact page numbers. Don't take anything to chance when you're making out your Christmas list.

I was totally satisfied with my family of baby dolls. Newcomers were always welcome though. I may have been barraged with television commercials and didn't even realize it. My eyes and heart settled on a toddler doll named Kissy. I had to have her. I couldn't wait to sniff her sweet new plastic smell. I marked her down on my list.

My mother looked at my letter to Santa.

"You only want two things this year?" she asked. She asked me to show her this carriage and doll in the catalog. I did and she pointed to a doll with brown hair next to Kissy on the page.

"What does this Kissy doll do? Wouldn't you rather have this pretty brown haired doll that drinks bottles and wets her diaper? she asked.

I looked at her like she was a bit slow.

"You press Kissy's arms together and she puckers her lips up and gives you a kiss. I don't want some brown haired doll peeing all over me, Mom. Why would I want a doll that pees all over me? This is pretend you know." I insisted.

I'm thinking right about then there was a brown haired peeing doll in a bag under her bed. Mom was thinking "Now, where did I put that receipt?"

Christmas morning came and my brothers and I bounced around the living room. I zeroed in on the red carriage. I rolled it back and forth a few feet in the small living room made smaller by the tree and all the gifts that spilled out from underneath it. Inside the carriage was a beautifully wrapped box.

My brother pointed out a shiny blue and silver girl's bicycle leaning against the wall. It was nice but there was a foot of snow out there. Santa brought me a bike?

I didn't even ask for a bike. I was mesmerized by the box that might contain Kissy.

It did! I lifted her from the packaging and breathed in deeply. She had the heady scent of perfumed rubber that all dolls made at the North Pole had. It made me dizzy breathing her in so deeply. I cradled her in my arms and I loved her completely.

My brother tried to point the bike out to me again. I waved him off and sat down to coo to my new Kissy doll. She was wearing a bright red and white checked pinafore. She had on shiny new red shoes. I pressed her arms together and she begged me for a kiss. I gave it to her. Over and over again.

Kissy was my new favorite. I wouldn't go anywhere without her.

My mother and Auntie were going to take me and my cousin to the movies. We were going to see a new movie called Mary Poppins. My mother told me Kissy had to stay at home.

"I am not going to have you forgetting something in that theater and making your aunt turn around. You are not taking anything with you. No dolls!" she said.

I really wanted to see Mary Poppins. I carried Kissy into the kitchen and stared my father down while he was drinking his coffee.

"What? he asked. "Why are you staring at me, Little Girl?" he asked.

"Mommy is taking me to the movies and she said there are no dolls allowed. I really want to see Mary Poppins but I need someone to watch Kissy. Will you watch her for me, Daddy? I know you don't think dolls are important. You didn't want to turn around and get my doll after the church picnic. I don't blame you because it was minutes out of your way. But, I guess what I'm saying is I want to leave Kissy with you and I think I might be able to trust you to watch her. But, I'm not sure." I finished one of the longest speeches I'd ever made.

"Sure, Little Girl. I'm not doing much today. Kissy can stay with me. I promise I'll watch her and she'll be just fine and dandy when you get back. Now, tell me. Who is this Mary Poppins and do you think she can really fly?" he wanted to know. So, I sat on his lap and told him.

Mary Poppins was wonderful! I hardly gave Kissy a thought. We arrived home and my father was making meatballs and sketti on the stove. Kissy was sitting on four pillows at my seat at the table. She had a plate of graham crackers in front of her and a little glass of milk.

My mother took one look at that doll sitting at the table and shook her head. She took our coats and hung them up in the closet. She came back into the kitchen and drained the pasta while my father asked all about the movie. Mom took Kissy and lay her down on the couch and covered her with a afghan while I told Daddy all about Mary Poppins and her umbrella.

As we ate our sketti and meatballs I thanked my father for watching Kissy.

"Someday you might have a little girl of your own." he said. "What will you name her?" he wanted to know.

"Kissy" I said with assurance.

My mother told me that was a doll's name. It was not a name for a real little girl. She said Kissy is nice but Chrissy is close. It's a real girl's name.

Chrissy.

"Yes, that's nice. I might name my real little girl Chrissy." I announced while I slurped up my sketti.

And I did.

****

Angel In New York City

I've visited New York City perhaps a dozen times in my life. I've felt it's heartbeat. I've smelled the fumes of too many cars. I've been jostled by the huge crowds. My ears have heard the cacophony of sounds. I liked it but I didn't.

I was used to a suburban setting. Streets that were empty at dinner time. Just the sound of one discontented dog barking. I knew where to find a crowd. I knew where to find silence.

I decided that New York City was one of those places that was "Nice to visit but I wouldn't want to live here."

It was December. I was a little girl and I belonged to a Brownie Troop. I proudly wore the almost empty sash. I attended weekly troop meetings. I found out that I was not crafty. I found out that I did not like learning pledges. I did like the other girls a lot though.

We sold calendars and wrapping paper. We were trying to earn enough for a bus trip to go to New York City. I'd never been there before. But, I heard it was the capital of the world!

I halfheartedly sold calendars. My mother bought a lot of overpriced wrapping paper and bows. Mom signed up to be a chaperone.

That surprised me.

She later told me "You wanted to go to New York City? I didn't trust anyone but me to keep their eye on you, Little Girl! I had no choice but to go along."

We got off the bus. The noises and smells assaulted us. We were herded into a group. We all went in to get a tour of NBC Studios. I remember the beautiful young bored interns that led us through the hallways.

I was unimpressed with a small room where Johnny Carson held court every night.

I did stop and spend many minutes in front of a very small lit up glass box. Inside lived the puppets that they had made Rudolph The Red Nosed Reindeer with. I couldn't believe how small they were. I wondered at the magic that must have happened to make them move. And sing. And capture our hearts.

My mother never tried to rush me. I thought she was pretty calm for a suburban housewife. Why wasn't she clutching her purse? Why wasn't she staring at the top of skyscrapers? Why didn't beggars on the street corners freak her out?

"I'm a city girl, Darlene. You didn't know me when I was a city girl. But...........there you have it." she explained to me as she brushed away a street person trying to touch my long auburn hair.

My mother was always teaching me lessons. I think she'd be surprised at how many I remember.

"If you were all alone...........a city girl............and someone tried to touch your hair. What would you do?" she asked me as we followed the group of Brownies down the street.

"I'd run?" I answered.

"No. You don't run. You use your voice. You use your voice all the way down in your belly. And, you yell. You say "Don't touch me! Stop touching me! You have no right to touch me!" There will be a hundred people around you. Ninety nine of them will walk on by. But, the hundredth person? Will come to help you. You just remember that. There are always angels among us." she counseled me on that busy sidewalk.

We followed the group of Brownies and their moms into a bright shining building. Huge soldier nutcracker figures guarded the sides of the entrance.

I found myself in F A O Schwartz.

My eyes grew big and round. I clutched my mother's hand as swarms of people passed us by. I had never imagined that such a place existed. Toys from around the world. Stuffed animals taller than I was. Trains circling around the ceiling. Dolls turning on pedestals.

My mother let go of my hand and opened her purse. She handed me a ten dollar bill.

My eyes widened at the sight of it. I had never held a ten dollar bill before.

"First of all...............put that in your pocket. Pat it. Let me see that you put it deep enough. That's what you have to spend. I hear we only have an half an hour so you can't take forever to decide what you want to buy. I also hear that Santa himself has been known to shop here. What would you like to buy?" asked my mother.

We let the swarms pass us by while I thought about it.

"I need to see the Barbie section." I replied. "Barbie clothes. Barbie clothes from New York City!"

"Okay, let's go find some sophisticated clothing for Barbie." my mother replied.

I didn't know what sophisticated meant, but I was in.

The huge corner dedicated to all things Barbie even took my mother's breath away.

I zeroed in a ballgown that would make Barbie look like a beautiful hummingbird. The dress was long and filmy. It was turquoise and blue and green with sparkles. It cost four dollars. Which was a mint for a doll outfit back then.

I told my mother to pick out an outfit also. I did that because she was the one that played Barbies with me day in and day out. She picked out a nurse's outfit for the doll.

I gave her a questioning look.

"Hey, a girl's got to make a living." she told me.

We paid at the register and stood near the door while the Brownie leader did a head count.

The day ended with a trip to Radio City Music Hall. We watched a long line of beautiful girls kick their legs over their heads. They held onto satin ropes and pretended to be reindeer. They pulled Santa in his sleigh.

We left that building and my mother asked me a question.

"So, do you want to be a Rockette someday?" she wanted to know.

"No." I replied.

I guess that wasn't enough for her.

"Why not?" she asked.

"They didn't even let those girls sing. Any dancer that makes it onto a stage in New York City can also sing. But, no! Just kick your foot over your head. You must be exactly this tall. You all have to be shaped exactly alike. I don't go for that Mom. Beautiful women come in all different sizes and shapes. And, they should be able to sing." I lectured her.

She threw her head back and laughed.

"So, all women don't need to look like Barbie?" she wanted to know.

"No, Mom. Barbie is a freak. We all know that. But, we love her anyways." I told her.

We had gone to an Automat for lunch before Radio City Music Hall. I stood in the busy room full of tables and brightly lit glass walls. My mother had to explain to me what it was I was seeing.

"All the glass boxes have food in them. You go up and put coins in the slot. You open the door and put the food on your tray. Now, I know this sounds like fun. Don't get carried away. I want you to eat what you take. Remember all the starving children in China." she said as she pushed me towards the sandwich with potato chip section.

We got sandwiches and chips and pickles. We got sodas to wash it down with. I wanted to plug a few nickles into the box with chocolate chip cookies but she told me no. Only if you have room in your stomach. After you finish your sandwich.

I was half way done with my ham and cheese sandwich. I had eaten all the chips. And, half a dill pickle as big as my hand. I needed to use the ladies room. The troop leader brought a few of us to do our business.

We got back to the table. My mother was in deep conversation with another Mom. They were discussing and laughing about how much wrapping paper they had to buy to get invited on this trip.

I stood behind my mother and tapped her on the shoulder. I tapped quite a few times to get her attention. I couldn't sit back down because there was a strange lady sitting in my seat.

The lady wearing all the clothes she owned at once was finishing my sandwich and soda. She was especially enjoying my pickle.

My mother finally responded to my tapping. I pointed towards the lady with the smudged face and the strange gloves without fingers.

My mother turned and gave the lady a look. I had received a 'scream from the bottom of your belly' lecture earlier on that day. I pursed my lips and half shut my eyes. I prepared for my mother to yell at the top of her lungs. I expected to hear "Do not eat my daughter's sandwich! Put down the pickle! Step away from the pickle!" perhaps.

Instead my mother stood up. She pushed me into her chair. She nodded to the other Mommy to watch me.

She gently touched the shoulder of the old lady dressed in rags. She spoke gently to her in a soothing voice.

"Come with me. Come with me to the wall. I think the meatloaf and mashed potato dinner looks luscious. Green beans with butter and a hot crescent roll. We can do better than a ham and cheese sandwich at Christmas time." she said to the woman.

The woman followed my mother to the wall of glass cubicles full of food that she couldn't touch because she had no money. My mother plugged quarters into the metal coin slot. She sat the woman down in my vacated chair and put the tray of food in front of her.

The woman put a forkful of meatloaf into her mouth. She shut her eyes in ecstasy. She looked up at my mother. My mother with the beautiful face. My mother with the long auburn hair twisted up into a bun. The red tendrils that framed her face. And, the big green eyes.

The lady spoke with her mouth full.

"I've heard of you, lady. I've heard that there are angels among us." the woman said.

****

Little Girl's Christmas

My name is Darlene. I have many nicknames. Most people call me Dar. My husband calls me Doodle. That nickname has spilled out into the rest of my life. My best friend calls Doodle Darla. My father in law called me Do-Dar. My daughter calls me her Doodler.

But, my parents? They called me Little Girl.

I accepted this name because it just was. I chaffed at it when I was a teenager. My father was 90 years old and he'd call me that in the grocery store. We got some strange looks. But, there was a time……………when I was just that.

I was a little girl. And, the name fit.

My parents called me Little Girl and it was right. My grandparents would call me Little Girl and it made me wonder.

"Do they know my real name?" I asked my mother.

"Of course they do. What a silly question. Why do you ask that?" my mother wanted to know.

"I can't explain it………………but, they are very, oh what's the word……………formal with me. When they call me Little Girl it is more like……………a description." I tried to explain to my mother.

I think I did a very good job of explaining since I was really……………still…………a little girl.

My mother thought about it. My mother never tried to blow off a difficult question just because it came from a child. Mommy Ellie always had a great respect for children and how they think.

"Well................they are formal people. They are Swedish and I think that makes them a little more stiff. You're used to my family. We're Irish and we're loud. We talk all the time and sing and dance and play. Your father's people aren't like that. But, just because they're quiet doesn't mean they don't love you." she explained as she put my hair into curlers.

Christmas Eve was coming. And, for some reason little girls had to have curly hair for Christmas.

"Also, I think there is something else going on there." my mother said. "Your grandparents have eleven grandchildren. Ten of them are boys. You are the only girl. Think of that! Time after time after time babies came home from the hospital. And, they were always boys. Until you. You are Little Girl to them."

"But, they do know your real name." she added as she snapped the last curler into place.

I awoke on Christmas Eve day and ran down the stairs early. I was not usually an early riser. But, I couldn't wait much longer for my mother to get those curlers out of my hair. They hurt. I skidded into the kitchen to find my grandfather drinking coffee with my parents.

This was not a regular occurrence. A big cardboard box full of wrapped Christmas gifts sat in the corner near the door.

It seems Grammy was sick. We weren't going to go and visit them on Christmas Eve night like usual.

This was not good. I was a little girl that liked her routines. Christmas Eve was supposed to happen at their house in Glastonbury. We would arrive just as it was getting dark. Grammy would have beautiful food arranged on platters in her little kitchen.

That little old fashioned kitchen................with the big free standing stove. The handmade cupboards that Grampy had made with oil cloth on the top instead of counter top. The same oil cloth was on top of the table and covered the floor.

The dining room would be all dressed up for Christmas. Grammy's maple hutch (that is mine now) would have bowls of candy sitting on top of the pretty doilies. The table would be set with lovely linen and special occasion dishes. Tweety Bird would chirp in his cage and spit seeds at us from the corner.

The skinny but tall artificial tree would greet us when we pulled up into their driveway. It was always in the same living room window. Old fashioned big bulbs lit it up in spectacular fashion.

My grandparents didn't decorate their tree with ornaments. Instead the branches were full of little presents for all of us. Wrapped in paper that was saved from year to year. Tied together and to the branches with big fat colorful yarn.

I ate whatever strange Swedish delicacies I had to…………..so I could get dessert. If you didn't eat your dinner? There was no dessert. Every Christmas Eve my grandmother would put a plate of her hollow cookies shaped like flowers right in front of me. They were full of her homemade raspberry jam and covered in powdered sugar.

"For Little Girl." she'd say as she placed that plate right in front of me.

That might be the only thing she said directly to me all evening………………but, in hindsight……………it was enough.

Grammy was sick? And, none of the above was going to happen. I was bereft as I sat quietly at the kitchen table with my parents and Grampy.

"She's got a horrible cold that settled into her throat. I took her to the doctor yesterday. He says it's something called strep and he gave her penicillin. But, he said she shouldn't be near anyone……………especially little girls…………..for the next few days. So she doesn't get little girls sick right before Christmas." Grampy said in my direction.

"My name is Darlene." I said quietly back in his direction.

Grampy gave me a strange look but he let it pass.

My mother cleared her throat and gave me the look. You know……………The Look!

"So, I brought over your box of presents, Little Girl." said Grampy. "Why don't we open them right now. I can't stay too long. I want to get back to your grandmother."

So, we all gathered in the little living room on Columbus Street to exchange gifts. I ran to my room to get the little wrapped can of snuff I had bought for Grampy.

I received hand knitted hats and mittens. And, slippers. My grandmother was an artist at knitting. The last present I opened wasn't soft. It was in a small box. I opened up a little glass doll. She had a sweet painted china doll face. She unscrewed at the waist. The little glass skirt was a perfume decanter.

It was the most perfect Little Girl gift ever.

My grandfather left. My mother scurried around and picked up the living room. She sent my father to the grocery store to buy a small ham and things to make her special scalloped potatoes since she now had to cook Christmas Eve dinner.

I did what I could to help in my Little Girl fashion. I ended up warming the television set up and watching most of It's A Wonderful Life.

The sun sets early in December. I looked out the window to see a few flakes of snow float by. It was a lazy snow. It was not a serious snow. It wasn't about to make anyone's Christmas. It was slow and depressing. It matched the way I felt.

My father sat at the little kitchen table. He drank coffee as my mother got the ham ready to go into the oven. She had a big pan of peeled potatoes sitting in water so they wouldn't turn brown.

"Well……………won't be the same. But, it will be kind of nice not to have to drive back and forth to Glastonbury tonight. We can just stay all cozy in our own little house." Daddy said to my mother. But, it was really me he was talking to.

That's when I remembered.

I had forgotten to bring my gift for my grandmother down when I had grabbed my Grampy's snuff.

My eyes flew open.

"Oh, no!" I wailed from the living room couch.

My Daddy came around the corner.

"What's the problem, Little Girl?" he asked in concern.

"I forgot to give Grampy my gift for Grammy. It's Christmas Eve and I always give her a gift. I bought it with my own money, Daddy. I bought her a beautiful pin. It looks like a wreath and it has red, white and green jewels in it. I know it's only glass but they look real. And, now………………she's sick……………and she thinks I didn't get her a present……………" I said as I started to cry and hiccup in dismay.

"How long until dinner, Ellie?" my father asked.

"Two hours, why? Oh, you're not driving all the way over there and back to drop off that pin. You can give it to her for New Years, Little Girl. She'll understand." my mother said as she stood in the doorway.

My father took one look at my face and said "Go get the present, Little Girl. Put on your coat and get in the station wagon. We'll be back in an hour, Ellie. We won't be stopping." said my Daddy as he grabbed his coat out of the hallway closet. "Call ahead and tell my father to answer the door when Little Girl rings the bell."

So, my dear wonderful Daddy drove me all the way to Glastonbury. The snow picked up a bit. It was no longer kidding around. This snow was here to decorate the landscape for Christmas Eve.

I sat in the front seat of the station wagon clutching that little gift. I can't explain why it was so important. Or, why my father recognized how important it was to me. I had picked out that pin myself. I had earned the money myself. And, I was just so sad that my Grammy was sick at Christmas. I was devastated that she might think I had forgotten about her on Christmas Eve of all days.

After all the Christmas Eves she had made so special for me.

My father pulled into their curving driveway. He parked his car near the big tree with the round picnic table built around it's trunk. I ran to the front door and rang the bell. My grandfather opened the door wearing the new green and black flannel shirt my mother had given him for Christmas. That would please her when I told her all about it.

"Hi, Grampy! Please, give this to Grammy. I bought it myself with my own money. I picked it out. I'm so sorry I forgot to give it to you earlier. Tell Grammy that I hope she feels better soon. Maybe she'll feel good enough to make my special cookies for New Years. Maybe she could teach me to make them someday." I said in a hurry as my breath painted circles around me.

"I'll tell her all that, Little Girl." my grandfather told me as he laughed.

And, that was the moment I figured it out. Why Little Girl sounded so funny coming from my grandparent's lips. It wasn't because it was a formal name to them. It wasn't because they didn't know my real name. It was because their slight Swedish accents made them hit the consonants too hard when they said the letter T and the letter G.

"Is Grammy up or is she in bed?" I asked as I climbed down the stairs.

"She is up. I'm about to feed her some dinner. I will tell her to take her pills with her coffee." said my grandfather.

"Tell her to go and stand next to Tweety Bird's cage, Grampy! So I can wave goodbye to her before I leave. Tell her when I wave it means Merry Christmas. Tell her God Jul!" I said as I ran down the path towards the driveway.

I got to the car and I stood in front of it.

"Daddy! Put on your lights! So Grammy can see me." I yelled in the direction of the station wagon.

Daddy did.

My grandmother appeared in the window. I could see Tweety's cage covered over for the night. She used the heel of her hand to clean the condensation off of the glass. I jumped up and down and waved. She waved back. I lie down flat on my back in the new snow. I made a snow angel for her. She clapped her hands together and waved some more.

I got into the front seat of the station wagon. My Daddy beeped the horn as we backed out of the winding driveway.

Daddy seemed a little choked up. "Well." he said as he sniffed. "Sometimes the best presents don't cost a penny. Right, Darlene?"

"My name is Little Girl." I answered.

****

Visiting Santa

There was once a little girl that was very curious. People said that she was kind of nosy. She really wasn't. She just wanted to know how things worked. Things and people.

She went to school every day. On Wednesdays the class was handed copies of a newspaper written for children. The little girl loved it. The newspaper used words and phrases she understood. It told her about the world around her. She learned about astronauts. She learned about the weather. She learned about different species of animals.

On the last page of every edition there was a small paragraph outlined in a box. It said "If you have a question for the editors please send it to such and such an address."

The teacher gave the class an assignment. All the children were to bring in an envelope and a postage stamp from home. The teacher handed them each a sheet of lined paper. The students were told to ask the editors anything they wanted to know.

It was early December. And, first and foremost on the little girl's mind was one big question.

"Is Santa Claus for real? And if he is? How does he get into houses that don't have chimneys? Please, answer before December 24th." wrote the little girl on the lined paper in her big block letters.

The letters were placed in their envelopes. The children licked the stamps themselves. Teacher promised to mail them the next day.

The teacher complimented the students on their very first letters. She said that the handwriting was very good. She was pleased with their questions. But, she gave them a warning.

"The editors of this newspaper are very busy people. I must warn you that you will not all receive an answer. That doesn't mean you didn't ask a very good question. I just wanted you to know that." she said to all the bright faces before her.

The little girl went to bed that night. She had a hard time falling asleep because she had so many things to think about.

She remembered what her Daddy said about that.

"If you have a hard time falling asleep you should count your blessings. Before you know it you will wake up in the morning. And, that is a blessing too." Daddy told her.

The little girl hugged her pillow. She loved her soft pillow. That was a blessing. Her warm comfortable bed was another. The gold kitty that lay next to her purring was yet another blessing. She smiled as she drifted off to sleep. All her curious questions could wait until the next day for answers.

The little girl had a very real dream.

She sat in front of an oak desk in a very pretty room. A fire crackled in the fireplace. A beautiful Christmas tree stood in a corner decorated with feathery angel ornaments. She sniffed at a bowl of sparkling pine cones.

They smelled like cinnamon and nutmeg and gingerbread men.

The door opened and a man entered. He was dressed in red velvet pants and a shirt with stripes like a candy cane. He straightened his hair and combed his white beard with his fingers.

He acted like he was about to meet someone very important.

"Ah, you're here!" he said to the little girl sitting in the oak chair in front of his desk. "That was quick. I was told to expect a reporter. I understand you have a very important question that needs to be answered before December 24th."

"As you know..........I'm pretty busy at this time of year. But, my Head Elf, Mortimer told me that it was very important to meet with you tonight. While you're asleep. While you're dreaming. The Head Elf told me that you are an important person. You have curiosity. You will someday be a writer. He told me that it is my job tonight to answer your questions." he said as he sat down.

The little girl stared at the man across the desk from her. She pinched the back of her hand. Yes, it hurt. Yes, she was awake.

"Who are you?" the little girl asked in a whisper.

"Speak up, child. I'm thousands of years old, after all. Please, don't be shy. I've been told you're curious if not down right nosy. Speak up nice and loud!" said the man with a big friendly chuckle.

His belly did indeed shake like a bowl full of jelly.

"I asked who are you?" the little girl said in a shout.

"Okay, that's your first question." said the jolly man. "Do you want to take notes? I do like to be quoted correctly. No? That's alright. No notes. I am Santa Claus. Saint Nicolaus. Kris Kringle. I have many names. But, I think you call me Santa."

"But, then you know that. Don't doubt what you're seeing and hearing, little girl. You're a smart one. You know your own mind. And, you also know what you believe. I'm kind of surprised by your written questions now that I've met you. You already know the answers. Please, don't let others tell you what to think. Don't let others tell you what to believe. You know in your heart what is real." Santa said as he laid his hand across his heart.

"I do?" asked the little girl.

"You do. You most certainly do." whispered Santa across the desk.

"I wanted to know if you were for real." said the little girl. "Now, I see with my very own eyes that you are! This room is real. I can feel it. I know it in my heart."

Santa leaned back in his swivel chair and smiled in satisfaction.

"And, your other question? I think it had something to do with chimneys." prompted the patient saint.

"Oh, yes! Chimneys! You are depicted up on the rooftop. You have a big bag of toys for the girls and boys. You lay a finger aside of your nose and whoosh! Down the chimney you go. That is your way of getting into houses. But! There are a lot of houses now adays that don't have chimneys! This has a lot of little girls and boys worried! How does that work?" asked the little girl.

She had grabbed a piece of paper and a pencil off of Santa's desk. This was an important question. She needed to write down the answer. She needed to get it just right.

"I don't need a chimney, dear child. I am happiness. I am hope. I am the wishes of all ages. I am the answer to prayers. I am the clouds that skid across the moon. I am the hush that comes with the new fallen snow at midnight. I am in the smile of little babies. I am in the laugh of the very old." Santa said in a very serious voice.

"Put down your pencil, little girl. And, look me in the face." said Santa.

"You are youth. You are childhood. But, as long as you believe your spirit will stay young forever. No matter how old you become. No matter how wrinkled your skin or how white your hair" he said as he leaned across the desk.

"I don't need a chimney, dear heart. Because? I am love. I am miracles. I am Christmas." he explained.

"But, then you already knew that. In your heart. While you drifted off to sleep with your favorite pillow. In your cozy bedroom. With your gold purring kitty by your side. You already knew the answer." said Santa Claus.

"Don't worry about chimneys, little girl. I am also magic!" said Santa as he twirled his hand in circles in front of her face. A sparkling red and white candy cane appeared in his hand. He presented it to the little girl with a flourish.

Little Girl awoke the next morning. She smiled and stretched and scratched her kitty underneath her golden furry chin.

Her hand then came down upon a sparkling red and white candy cane that rested on the bedspread. Next to it lay notes taken in her block lettered handwriting.

The little girl stopped worrying about chimneys.

****

A Cat's Christmas

I love Christmas decorations. I always have. I would bug my mother to put up the tree on Columbus Street days before she was ready.

She put me off by telling me that she wasn't about to decorate a "dirty" living room. That room was never dirty. What she meant was it would be polished to a shine before she added anything to the décor.

She would hand me a tin can of furniture polish and a soft old rag.

"Get to work, Little Girl. Shine up the curliques on the front window table. Get into the little wooden flowers on the bottom of the desk. Use your muscles. Then get out the newspaper and Windex that front window.   Then we'll talk about decorating for Christmas." she'd say.

I'd sigh and get to work. You can't display your Christmas decorations in a "dirty" room. It was the rule. I tried to circumvent that rule every year. I never succeeded.

I now own myriad plastic tubs full of decorations. My house is of average size. I like to say I own enough Christmas stuff to decorate a huge Victorian house. I no longer bring out all the decorations at once like a did as a newlywed. My collection has expanded to the extent that

I rummage through and just bring up what I need from the basement.

The porcelain village and it's inhabitants make it up the cellar stairs every other year. It takes hours to display all that stuff correctly. My kids are grown up. They don't help anymore through lack of interest or the fact that one lives thousands of miles away.

The only one willing to help is the cat. She has a knack of lying in the middle of the box I want to delve into. She rearranges sheets of fabric that are manufactured to look like a landscape of snow. She grabs elves made of pine cones and hides them under the couch.

She wants to lick them later when she has a free hour.

Certain ornaments are really too ratty looking to display any longer. That doesn't stop me. Because they are full of memories. I look at a lopsided pipe cleaner tree and I remember the person that made it. I even have a tiny plastic nativity scene that my grandparents gave me when I was six years old. That sits on a branch of the tree every year.

My mother had a small tree made out of feathers when I was a little girl. She put it on an end table in the living room next to her nativity scene. The nativity was rustic. The light green tree with it's soft plumage and small gold glass balls was glitzy. I never thought they went well together but she loved it.

She loved that little feathered tree because her mother had given it to her. For her nativity scene.

It stood about a foot tall and was quite gorgeous to look at. The feathers were very soft to the touch. It didn't light up but it didn't need to. It was that beautiful.

I was allowed to pet it a few times a season when I was a little girl. Under adult supervision. It was to look at not to touch I was told over and over again. I reverently touched it all I wanted when no one was looking of course.

The year I was ten we added a beautiful gold angora cat to the family. Goldie didn't climb Christmas trees. Goldie didn't jump on the table when people were eating. Goldie did her business outside. Goldie was a very friendly, loving and well behaved feline

But, Goldie would not leave that feathered Christmas tree alone. I witnessed my mother fight with that yellow cat for a month. And, it was all about that tree made of feathers.

Mom caught Goldie sitting in the middle of the manger scene. Cats are adept at sitting on anything at any height without knocking anything over. Mary was right where she should be. Joseph stood next to her looking worried.

Baby Jesus lay in his crib waving his hands. I think Jesus was afraid that big golden cat was about to suffocate him.

But, Goldie was dainty. She never messed around with the Holy Family. She just wanted to be close to that feathered tree.

She nuzzled it. She stroked the soft feathers with her chin. She smiled and purred and loved the world when she was close to that tree. Then she started to salivate. She licked a feather. And, she licked some more.

"Ma? You'd better come in here. I think this tree must be made out of dead canaries or something. Goldie is licking it! She's purring really loud and weird. Her butt is wiggling back and forth! I tried to stop her but she got up on her hind legs and hissed at me. She's in some kind of frenzy." I yelled from the living room.

My mother came from around the corner with a dish towel in her hand. My mother always had a dish towel in her hand. She twisted the towel into a weapon. She snapped it at the cat. She connected with Goldie's butt. The cat jumped halfway across the room and yowled at the door.

My mother opened the front door and helped Goldie out with a nudge of her foot.

"What the heck was that all about?" my mother whispered at the room.

"It was like that time you gave her a catnip mouse. And, she got all weird and excited. She got so excited she pissed herself." I remembered.

"Don't say 'pissed', Little Girl. She got so excited she URINATED on herself." my mother corrected me.

"Pissed is a much better word." I said.

"Yes, you're right." my mother murmured as she watched Goldie run at the maple tree in the front yard and climb it without even trying.

"Let that cat settle down before you let her back in." my mother told me as she headed to the kitchen. "If she goes near my mother's feathered tree again you let me know. This is not up for discussion. I will not have that cat tearing apart my mother's Christmas tree."

I was on guard in that living room quite often. I was fond of reading a book while curled up under the tree. But, I did have to go to school. I did have to sleep once in a while.

And, come on. There is no outsmarting a cat when they are intent on something. And, Goldie was intent on loving up that feathered Christmas tree.

The war between Goldie and my mother went on for the month of December. Mom would put the tree up on the mantlepiece. The cat jumped up there and softly stepped around porcelain cherubs and polished candlesticks. She'd head bump that feathered tree until it fell onto the living room rug. There she would body press it with all of her weight.

My mother would discover this scenario. She got hissed at by an ordinarily loving cat. This was a war and Goldie brought out her hisses and her claws. My mother took to hissing right back.

Goldie didn't seem to understand English like she used to. No amount of "What a good girl. Goldie has her own toys. Now, leave my tree alone sweet little girl." got through to her. The hissing coming past my mother's lips? Goldie understood that.

She hissed right back and ran at my mother. Full speed. She climbed up her legs covered in black stretch pants. She went for her face.

I just put my book down and rolled around the living room rug laughing myself silly.

"You think this is funny?" my mother screeched at me. "Go grab that crazy cat and get her the hell out of my house. She can freeze her butt off on the back step all night for all I care. This is MY house. And, that is MY tree.

It's snowing like hell out there. Let's see how feisty she is when she's sleeping in the snow tonight. Get that cat the HELL OUT OF MY HOUSE!"

I asked Goldie nicely to leave and she did.

My mother was too soft hearted to leave our cat in the snow all night of course. She'd glance out the kitchen window every twenty minutes or so during the early evening hours. She talked to the closed door.

"You crazy cat! You think you're the boss of me? You think you can lick my tree? You think it's yours? Well, I don't think so! You can freeze your furry little butt off for all I care. Go ahead, Cry. Cry all you want. You're not getting in this house tonight. You crazy little thing." she said as she paced the kitchen.

I'd go to say something but she'd shut me up.

"Zip it, Little Girl. Or, you can go sit on the back step with your precious tree eating cat." she snapped at me.

My father came home from the second shift at Pratt and Whitney. He didn't know the extent of the cat/tree war. He tried to get the cat to come in out of the snow. Goldie wouldn't shift.

I think she was that mad at my mother.

My father was a cat loving man. He tried to get the cat to come in a number of times. He was tired. He wanted to go to bed. He made a bed from a soft old blanket in the corner of the garage. He put Goldie's food and water out there with her. He threw the cat in the garage and he went to bed.

Goldie stayed there for days. She was protesting. If she had been able to write? She would have been out there composing signs on placards.

"Unfair Cat Practices!" "Down With Bossy Housewives!" "Feathered Trees Were Made For Cats!" If Goldie could write really small? I imagine a sign that would say "Hey Woman! I Only Keep You Around Because You Know How To Open Cans". I can imagine that sign bobbing up and down outside the kitchen window.

Christmas was coming. The manger scene was intact. The feathered tree however was no longer beautiful. It had been well loved by a cat. It had been licked at while we all slept. It was scraggly. It drooped. It leaned to the left.

Our house on Columbus Street now had a bedraggled but beloved feather tree. But, it was a house without a cat on Christmas Eve.

My mother was missing her cat. She missed her purring friend that helped her turn the pages of her newspapers well into the night. There was no feline blinking at her while she drank her hot tea. There was no furry creature to share her pillow with at night.

The Christmas Eve company had gone home. A plate with cookies and a glass of milk sat near the fireplace. My eyes were drooping and I was ready to say goodnight. Santa can't come if you're still awake.

My mother stood at the kitchen window staring at the garage. My father had installed a little lamp out there for Goldie.

"Screwy cat. Okay, you win." Mom said to the darkened window.

Mom opened the basement door. She started dressing in the old long woolen coat she hung laundry in. She put a red knitted hat on her head. She took a long scarf and wrapped it mostly around her face. She wasn't looking for warmth. She was protecting herself against an angry stubborn cat.

"Darlene! I'm going out there and coming back with that crazy cat. When I kick at the back door open it and get out of our way." my mother said as she marched towards the garage

I shook my head to awaken myself. I stood up straight and tall at the kitchen door. I tensed my muscles as I clutched the door knob. I was ready.

My mother was back in two minutes. She kicked the door and I made it fly open. Mom deposited a soft old blanket on the floor. Goldie wriggled out of it as my mother hung her outdoor clothing up on the hooks at the back of the basement door.

Goldie went to the corner of the kitchen between the stove and the cupboards. That is where her food dishes usually lived. She looked my mother in the face. She looked at the empty floor where her dishes should be. She opened her mouth wide and yawned all the way down to her tail.

At least the cat wasn't a gloating winner.

Mom placed a plastic Christmas placemat on the floor. She took out a bowl and filled it with water. She grabbed a saucer and put a whole can of cat food onto it. She hummed Jingle Bells the whole time she prepared Goldie's Christmas Eve dinner.

Goldie stared unblinkingly at the woman the whole time. She did blink her eyes in contentment when the tuna dish hit the floor. She took the time to twirl around my mother's ankles before she dove into the dish of fish.

I used the bathroom. I took a hot bath. I brushed my teeth. I threw my dirty towel down the basement stairs.

I went through the living room to climb the stairs to my bedroom. My father lay on the couch with his hands clutched to his chest. His snores were aimed at the ceiling. My mother sat in her reading chair with her newspaper. Goldie lay on the back of the chair nibbling at the tendrils of hair that escaped my mother's bun.

The fire was dying down in the fireplace. The Christmas tree blinked in the corner. The stockings hung empty from the mantlepiece. Santa was surely on his way. I glanced at a small log that hissed and shifted position in the fireplace.

That's when I noticed that there was already a gift under the tree.

It was a soft light green feathered Christmas tree ornament about a foot tall. The big tag stuck to it's base said "To Goldie, Love, Ellie."

****

Bourbon Balls

My Daddy went to make his lunch to take to work. He opened the kitchen cupboard and was met by an empty box of Twinkies. There was no dessert in the house to add to his sandwich and pickles. He looked kind of sad.

The next day I wanted to make my father a surprise. I was ten years old and I decided I was old enough to bake. I told my mother I wanted to make cupcakes for a surprise for Dad.

She dug through the cupboard and found me a cake mix. She set out some measuring cups, some eggs , oil and a hand beater. She watched me make a mess from the kitchen table while she sipped tea and flipped through a newspaper.

She supervised the cupcake tins going in and out of the oven. She put oven mitts on my hands and saw that I had sense enough not to burn myself. She was satisfied and never baked again.

It was now my job to keep the Tupperware dessert container full.

Christmas was coming and I was pumping out the Spritz cookies. Sprinkles and powdered sugar were flying all around the kitchen. My mother put those cookies away into tins. They were being saved for family celebrations and tea with her friends.

My father had a party at work. Everyone in his department at Pratt and Whitney were going to bring food to share to celebrate the season. The rules had just been changed and alcohol at company parties was forbidden. My father found a way around that rule.

He came home a few days before that party and handed me a recipe. It said Bourbon Balls at the top. The list of ingredients wasn't that long. The recipe said it made two dozen one inch Bourbon Balls.

"It's a big party, Darlene. I need you to triple that recipe. You're doing pretty good with your fractions. I think you can figure it out" he said as he patted me on the head messing up my hair. He handed me a bottle of Bourbon from the package store.

"And, no tasting that stuff!" he added. "It's strong alcohol and it will make you sick."

I sniffed it in appreciation. I now associate that smell with Christmas.

I set to work. First I sat down with a red colored pencil and paper and did my math. I transcribed the recipe and tripled it.

It was a no bake cookie recipe. The dough was so pungent with alcohol it made my eyes water. I rolled the balls in my hands and lined 70 of those little beauties up on waxed paper. The last step was to roll them in coconut. The coconut was the only thing keeping them from sticking together.

I tasted one as every good cook should. It made me feel a little fuzzy. Like I wanted to lay down someplace warm and go to sleep. I felt like Julia Childs sounds.

I put them in a pretty Christmas gift box lined with waxed paper. None of my mothers cookie tins were big enough. You could smell the bourbon wafting from that box all the way into the living room.

The next night my father went to work taking the cookies with him. He was gone. The cookies were gone. But, you could still smell them. I think the fragrance was now embedded in the curtains.

I heard him telling my mother the next day about the party. The guys didn't have to do much work. They had raffles and games and of course the big buffet meal.

"Oh, Ellie. The dessert table was wonderful. You've never seen such a spread. But, guess what went first? What everyone was raving about? Darlene's Bourbon Balls! Al from Accounting had four of them. He was bouncing off the walls. My boss's secretary had a few and she was giggling in the corner like a crazy thing. It was the best company party ever!"he declared.

I deciphered that conversation. I had made people drunk! I remembered my warm fuzziness. Oh, my God! I must have done my math wrong. I sat down again and worked the numbers. I had not tripled the bourbon. I had bourboned them times six!

New Years rolled around. My father was excited. The work Christmas party had been such a hit that everyone was willing to cook and bake again for New Years. He came at me with another bottle of Bourbon and a glint in his eye.

I took my transcribed recipe out of the box. I pointed at the numbers written in red colored pencil.

I said, "I am so sorry I messed up my math last time, Daddy. I made a mistake multiplying 1/4 cup of bourbon times three. Daddy! I made the bourbon times six by mistake. That's why they were so stinky and your friends all got drunk eating them. I won't make that mistake this time. I'll do it right this time. I promise."

He took my recipe and gave it a good look. On the left was the original recipe. On the right was my math tripling it. He found the glaring error.

He pointed to the wrong amount of Bourbon and said "Don't you fix a thing. You do it exactly as you wrote it down. Some of the greatest inventions ever invented were nothing but mistakes." he said with a smile.

"And, phew! Your Bourbon Balls! One of the best mistakes mankind has ever tasted!"

****

Goldie

According to my mother; she didn't like cats. We always owned one though. We lived in a subdivision of small cape cods. They were close together and I think from time to time someone would dump a load of kittens. There always seemed to be a cat meowing around the neighborhood looking for a home.

We adopted Goldie off the streets when I was about ten. My mother put up a four day fight because she said she was "allergic" to felines. It didn't bother her breathing but she said her skin would break out. She said that gold angora cat would give her hives.

Eventually the cat made it into the house, into our lives and into my heart at least. She slept with me and kept me company. She had the absolute loudest purr of any cat I've ever met. That purr was great to fall asleep to.

My mother took good care of her. She fed her and kept the litter clean. She arranged care when we'd go away for a week. But, she would hardly touch her. Once in a while I'd catch her scratching her head with the tip of an index finger muttering "What a good girl, what a good girl." Then she would go soap up her hands and dry off with a paper towel.

December 1973 brought a terrible ice storm. We were without power for a week. My parents kept the house from freezing by using the fireplace in the living room. It was a fireplace that was probably installed to have a pretty fire once in a while. That week it got a work out.

Three nights after losing power my mother woke me up by shaking me. She said she had to shake me for minutes to get me to come to. She repeated it with my brothers. She had called 911 and we grabbed the cat and went outside into the cold as the house was full of smoke.

The ornamental fireplace had caught fire inside the wall. The volunteer fire department came. They ripped out that pretty maple mantlepiece. They used axes and knocked down most of the wall at the end of the house. They sprayed white foam over everything in that room.

We didn't get power back for a few more days. My father kept the house livable by borrowing a friend's kerosene heater. We all cheered a few days later when we saw a lineman hooking power back up outside the house.

We put the house back together as best we could. Christmas was coming after all. I walked by my mother one night on my way to bed. She was sitting in her chair where she enjoyed her newspapers every night while we slept.

Usually, Goldie was laying across the back of the chair. My mother would put a dish towel at the back of her neck so she wouldn't get "cat hives." That night Goldie was lying in her lap and my mother was open hand petting her. Taking the dislodged fur and blowing it off her hand.

"Do you still say prayers at night, Darlene?" she asked as I put a foot on the bottom stair.

I stopped and said, "Um, sometimes. Not as often as I should, but yes I say my prayers."

"When you say your prayers tonight I want you to thank God for sending Goldie to us. She saved us all the other night. She jumped on me in bed and wouldn't stop swatting me in the face until I woke up." she said as she held Goldie's paw in her hand. She was gazing at her adoringly.

It was then that I noticed the red rash and the scratches on my mother's face.

****

Auntie Maneuvers

I've lived a blessed life. I've always been rich. Oh, I'm not talking about dollars lined up in a row. I'm talking about people. People that loved me.

I'm here to talk about aunties. I was rich in aunties. I had so many of them we ran out of names. Or, that's what I thought when I was a little girl.

My mother had sisters and sister-in-laws that shared names. I eventually figured it all out. I almost needed a map. But, I got to know them all and could tell who my mother was talking about pretty quickly.

I had fun aunties. And stern aunties. Some looked like me. Some didn't. But, they all had one thing in common. They all stole moments to be with me. Just with me.

An auntie would be visiting at Christmas. A coat would get thrown at my head. "Put that on." she'd say. "We're going for a walk." My mother would groan that dinner was almost ready. That auntie was a stern one. "We're going for a walk, Ellie. I'm going to get this girl to tell me all your secrets."

And, off we'd go for a walk. Stern Auntie didn't pump me full of questions. She'd only been teasing her little sister. She just wanted to hold my hand and walk around the block while the snow fell onto our eyelashes.

That auntie was quiet but she made a memory with me.

I had many fun aunties. The ones that would float on a tube with me for hours in Lake Champlain. The ones that would blow smoke in my face as they told me what a brat my mother had been at my age. The ones that gave me sips of their wine coolers. The one that told me to go into the house and ask my mother if she could still burp the whole alphabet at once. The one that was forever telling my mother to "lighten up" as she slipped me dollar bills.

Fun aunties. These ladies all belonged to my mother's side of the family.

My Daddy came with a trio of sisters all his own. I didn't see them as much because they lived further away. They all came for a yearly visit. These aunties emanated love. I would find them gazing at me adoringly. I'd done nothing to earn this adulation. It just was.

"Come and stand in front of me." one of Daddy's sisters would say. "Oh, my God! You look just like my mother when she was a girl. Do you sing? My mother has a beautiful voice. You must be a singer."

"Yes, I sing." I'd answer as I tried to pull away from the lady that loved me. The one that I really didn't know.

"Sing for me." she'd say. She really meant it. I could tell a song would really mean the world to her. My mother would harumph behind me. She was afraid that my natural nasty teenager personality was going to ruin this moment. I had to prove my mother wrong of course. As any thirteen year old girl should. I opened my mouth and sang.

"Let there be peace on earth……………and let it begin with me…………..let there be peace on earth……………the peace that was meant to be……………with God as our Father…………..brothers all are we………………" I sang until I went past my big money notes.

I looked around the little kitchen when the song was done. My mother looked surprised. She thought maybe I could sing…………..but she hadn't heard my voice in years. Three aunties from Maine sat sipping coffee with tears rolling down their faces.

One auntie played let's make up a story games with me from the time I was a little girl. She'd pull me onto her lap. She'd say "I want you to tell me a story. I will give you the first line and we'll see what you come up with." I think she played this game with all her nieces and nephews.

She'd give me a fantastical first line to a story and I would continue. I'd continue for a few good minutes. I remember her looking surprised. She turned me around on her lap and said "Oh, my goodness. We have a storyteller here. We finally have our writer. Write down our family stories some day, Little Girl. You'll be our hero."

Sometimes proximity is what makes the heart grow fonder.

My favorite auntie lived the closest. She was just a fifteen minute car ride away. I knew her the best because I saw her the most. She was also one of my mother's closest friends. They spoke for an hour on the phone every day. So, I suppose whatever I got up to at any age was discussed at length.

She knew me quite well. And, still she loved me.

This auntie had many special talents. She was a terrific housekeeper. She bought great things at the grocery store. Like Fritos. She was a master with a slow cooker. The smells coming out of her kitchen made your stomach growl hours before that slow cooker dinged.

She asked way ahead of time what you wanted for your birthday. What did you want for Christmas? And, then she actually purchased whatever silly thing your heart desired. She was a natural decorator. So, the wrapping on those gifts was so beautiful you didn't want to destroy it to see what was inside. It was sort of like a cake that is too pretty to cut.

If you were thirteen and got mad at your mother? And, you unloaded on this auntie? She zipped her lip and kept your secrets.

This auntie also had a super duper talent. She knew how to drive. She had a driver's license and a big roomie car.

She was always up for driving us anywhere that someone knew how to get to.

Every once in a while she'd get sick of sitting alone in her apartment while her husband worked. She'd show up at our house for a meal and a good long gossip session with my mother. If it got dark out.................she'd spend the night

She was terrified to drive after dark.

So, she was also the cool sleepover auntie.

Christmas was coming. I sat reading in the corner chair in the living room. The fireplace was toasting my feet. The Christmas tree was blinking in the other corner. I was content to read and listen to the female voices coming from the kitchen.

My mother and auntie must have gotten tired of the hard kitchen chairs. They came into the living room and deposited themselves onto soft cushions. They enjoyed the quiet of the flames for a moment. And, then they interrupted my reading.

"What are you reading?" asked Auntie.

"A Christmas Carol by Charles Dickens." I answered as I put the book down on my lap. I knew reading time was over.

"A Christmas Carol? Isn't that Scrooge?" asked my mother. "I think that movie is on tonight."

She was trying to get rid of me.

I'd seen that movie at least ten times.

"I prefer the book." I answered. There would be no getting rid of me.

My auntie then told me that I wasn't getting what I had asked for that Christmas.

"I know you wanted that green sweater with your initials on the front. But, when it came in the mail………….it was the most God awful green. I can't explain it to you. It wasn't neon green. It wasn't granny smith apple green. It was baby poop green. I had to send it back. It was just awful. But, I'll get you something nice." she said.

"I'm sure you'll get me something beautiful, Auntie. Don't worry about it." I said as I tried to pick my book up again.

They didn't swat the book out of my hand. But, the ladies just weren't having this reading thing going on in the corner.

"You'll never believe what happened today!" said Auntie.

"What happened today?"I asked as I shut the book and put it on top of the bookcase.

"Your mother and I went to Shady Glen for lunch. We both got those cheeseburgers with the fried curled up cheese on them. Your mother was talking. I've told her a million times not to try to talk with her mouth full." explained Auntie.

My mother grimaced at being described as the lady that talks with her mouth full.

This was getting good.

"And, then what happened?" I prompted her because she almost stopped talking at the look on my mother's face.

"Well! She was laughing and telling me something while she took a big mouthful of their delicious cole slaw. And, she started choking. Coughing and sputtering and tears rolling down her face. It was just awful!" my aunt described.

My mother put her head onto the back of the couch and stared at the ceiling. This was a sister-in-law after all. You can tell your sister to just shut up. But, not your sister-in-law. No matter how friendly you are.

"I asked her three times if she could breathe. I was petrified she was choking. I was standing behind her ready to give her the hymen maneuver when she started talking. She was still coughing but she was gasping out

"I'm okay, I'm okay." my aunt proclaimed the big news of the day.

I bit my top lip. I loved these ladies. I didn't want to make fun of them. I had sex-ed classes in school. I know for a fact that the nuns that taught them when they were thirteen years old had skipped over that whole sex thing.

"You stood behind her and did what, Auntie?" I asked quietly.

My mother hadn't blinked an eye. So, she had no idea that Auntie was using the wrong word.

"I almost had to do the hymen maneuver. I was never so scared in my life!" screeched my auntie as she remembered that afternoon's terrifying moment.

I took a little sip of my hot chocolate at that moment. Bad idea. I heard "hymen maneuver" a second time and a little liquid chocolate shot out of my nose.

I mopped myself up with a paper napkin that had held two cookies.

"Have you told this story to anyone else today?" I asked my innocent auntie. The auntie that was so tiny her little feet never touched the floor when she sat down in my Daddy's recliner.

"Well, I told your uncle all about it when he called to tell me that he was working a double shift. He just laughed and snorted at me and hung up on me. I really think he has an awfully strange sense of humor. He thinks it's funny that his sister almost choked to death on coleslaw and that I almost had to save her? Sick. Sick. I think he's working too much. He needs to take a day off." she said in a huff.

I put my hand over my lips. I tugged and tugged at the smile that was forming. I bit my bottom lip. I didn't want to laugh in this savior's face. My little auntie that was willing to bear hug my mother back into life. In time to save Christmas.

"Well……………………I'm thinking the phrase you're really looking for is Heimlich Maneuver." I told my auntie. "The Hymen Maneuver is really ……………well, let's say………………that's something entirely different."

I got up and went to the little bookshelf under the corner window. I grabbed the big fat Webster's Dictionary from the bottom shelf. I sat on the floor in front of Auntie and I flipped through the H's.

I found the word hymen. I put the big fat book that weighed almost as much as she did on her lap. I kept my forefinger on the word that she needed to see.

She read the definition. Her eyes grew wide. Her pure alabaster skin turned an alarming shade of mottled red. She stared me in the eyes. I gave her a little smile back. She started swinging her feet around in circles. She put her head back and she howled with laughter.

Now, my mother felt left out.

"What? What? What's so funny? What's so funny about me almost choking to death?" she screeched from the long sofa.

This had my auntie roaring even louder.

I got up and brought the dictionary over to my mother. I put it on her lap. I handed her reading glasses to her. She perched the glasses imperiously on her nose. She looked down through the lenses to read the definition of hymen.

My mother looked up in shock. She looked down again. I guess she didn't believe what she was reading the first time. The second time it sunk in.

She looked at my auntie and they roared. They were bent over. They were gasping for breath. I stood at attention as I laughed with them. The laughing was so overwhelming I didn't know if I was going to have to spring into action. Splash some cold water on them. Give them a slap across the face.

It was that intense.

They finally sputtered out to a few giggles and guffaws.

"You didn't tell anyone else, did you?" my mother finally gasped out in my aunt's direction.

My aunt thought about it.

"Only the mailman!" she screeched before she hit the floor and started rolling.

My mother laughed with her. She lie down on the couch. Her legs kicked. Eventually her head was almost on the floor because her sneakers were kicking at the white living room wall.

I just got out of their way. I closed the dictionary and put it back into it's place.

That's when my father walked through the front door and asked them "What's so funny?"

****

Christmas Shopping With My Mother

I am a solitary shopper.

I learned early on that shopping with friends doesn't work out for me. I would come home and model new clothing all alone in my bedroom when I was a teenager. I would be appalled at what my friends had talked me into buying.

I couldn't believe what I was seeing in the mirror.

I knew I'd never wear the jeans with the butterflies crawling all over my butt. A red shirt with rhinestones on the cuffs. What the heck? It would all go back to the store.

I'd return all the merchandise and replace it with things that didn't make my eyes water.

I earned my own spending money from the age of twelve. I had a paper route because I didn't like to baby sit. Babies terrified me. The few times I got talked into it..........I ended up sitting with a little boy that would scream "No, you She Devil!" every time I came near him. A one year old girl that banged her head against the crib...........her mother said it was her way of pacifying herself.

I told that mother to buy the kid a helmet. I never went back.

I got myself a paper route.

My mother gave up hope that I'd ever give her grandchildren.

But, there was a pair of ladies that I did like to shop with. Oh, I wouldn't actually buy anything when I was with them. I was there for the show. I tagged along for the entertainment.

I was sixteen and got a job at a local take out restaurant. Christmas was coming. My mother all of a sudden got interested in my work schedule.

"Write down on the calendar when you have to work." she told me. So, I did. I knew what she was up to. I had just gotten my driver's license. My mother and her best friend didn't drive. I was going to be their chauffeur.

"I'd like to book you for Wednesday and Thursday nights this week. To drive me and Rose to Grants. We want to do our Christmas shopping without men breathing down our necks. Men hurry us. You won't hurry us.............will you? I am your mother after all. I gave birth to you. You weighed ten pounds. It hurt like hell...............so I figure you can take us shopping and have some patience. If we get it all done on Wednesday ....we'll take you to the new Chinese restaurant for dinner on Thursday."she said.

My mother could always make me laugh like hell. Especially, when she wasn't trying to be funny.

"I can take you two shopping I suppose. Is this where I hear about your stretch marks? What was it, Ma? Eighty...........ninety hours of labor? Really. I don't need the dramatic stories. I am perfectly happy to drive you and Rose to Grants. And, I won't rush you. " I added as she glared at me.

You would have given them a ride too. Rose and my mother were like hanging out with Laurel and Hardy. Abbott and Costello. The closest comparison is probably Lucy and Ethel.

My mother Ellie was a statuesque beauty. 5'9" tall with amazing dark auburn hair. Big green eyes. A quick smile. A laugh she liked to share. She carried herself like a monarch.

Rose was like a tiny little bird. She might be only four and a half feet tall…………but she added another foot in height with her teased black hair. She had the softest most melodic voice. Cats would run to her and rub against her ankles when she spoke. She was tiny so she always wore high heels. No matter what she was doing…………..she clicked around on stiletto heels.

I asked her once at a picnic……………."Don't your feet hurt in those shoes?" She answered "I haven't felt my feet since 1948, honey. Go and get me some more deviled eggs."

So, on Wednesday night I pulled into Grants parking lot. I took up two spaces. I didn't mean to, but that's how bad I was at parking when I first started driving. The ladies exited the station wagon clutching their purses.

They each had a glint in their eyes.

Grants had started out as a good old fashioned Five And Dime store. It still housed the original luncheonette with it's red vinyl stools. All the waitresses were original too. Original hair nets. The store was becoming a "department store". The line of merchandise expanded every year.

This was an old fashioned store. The kind you'd like to go back and revisit if you could. Things weren't displayed on shelves. Everything was laid out on huge tables with shelving on the sides. It smelled like popcorn. The front windows were hidden by stacks of things for sale and by bucking bronco kiddie rides that ran on a dime.

The two women always started out sharing a cart. I pushed. I was the purse guard. They each had a little notebook. They flipped them open. Names were listed with amounts next to the name. They were on a budget. They used only cash so this was important.

Each of these women were in possession of at least one of those new fangled credit cards. But, their men had them terrified of actually using them.

I witnessed my father giving my mother her credit card. We sat at the little maple table in our kitchen. He pushed the red and white square of plastic towards her. But, he wouldn't take his big square finger off of it until he'd given her the "Evils of Credit Cards" speech.

This speech included phrases like …………..fifteen percent interest…………only in an emergency…………..selling my soul to the devil……………if you use this I will burst into flames. No matter where I am. I'll be nothing but a small pile of ashes.

Yes, my father could get quite dramatic.

So, these two ladies jotted down prices. They added tax. Because they were going to pay with cash at that register.

They filled that cart in an half an hour. They were completely done with their shopping that fast.

Oh, I wasn't fooled. Things had just started.

This is when they would continue looking around. Just because it felt good to get out of the house. Just because the store was so brimming and shining for Christmas. Because they had a chauffeur that wasn't rushing them.

This is where they would start to change their minds. Things would get put back. Then they'd return to pick those items up again.

I talked them out of the velour shirts. Velour was brand new. I know how enticing it is to touch. I know how velvet like it is. But, I knew the men in my life were not going to wear almost velvet shirts. I told them their original choice of flash lights was a much better bet.

That's when we picked up the store detective.

My two women stiffened up. They whispered to each other.

They were being followed.

This female store detective was an original too. She'd been hired right along with the now gray haired waitresses. I remembered her from when I was a little girl being pushed around this store in a cart. I would be covered with purses and coats and boxes of Whitman's Samplers. Even I knew her face.

I turned to the store detective. I was all grown up now. I had a driver's license. I felt pretty protective of my women.

"They're not stealing you know. They're just indecisive. On a budget. They're going to change their minds ten times because.............I'm not rushing them. We're going to take a break in about an hour. Meet you over in the luncheonette? We'll buy you a grilled cheese and tomato soup." I said to the woman skulking behind the display of woolen socks.

The woman grinned at me.

"Look at you all grown up! Meet you three ladies in the luncheonette in an hour. Tell your mother that the red light specials are about to start up." she said as she left to skulk around someone else.

A red light on a tall pole lit up and spun around like the beacon on an ambulance. A voice came over a loudspeaker.

"Hello, Christmas shoppers! For ten minutes only.................our red light special is in the Men's Department. Fruit of the Loom heavy sweatpants for all the men in your life! Keep your men warm when they're out shoveling snow this winter! Only $1.00 a pair for the next ten minutes!" said the disembodied voice on the loudspeaker.

Mom and Rose ran for the red light.

I walked.

I came around the corner and witnessed my mother and a big lady wearing a men's flannel shirt in a tug of war. Between them was a stack of men's sweatpants sized X-tra large.

The competition was on.

"Mom. Mom? Mom!!! What do you need with eight pairs of gray sweatpants. One pair is enough. Let go. Step away. Let the lady have a pair of sweatpants, Ma!" I shouted in my mother's ear.

Boy, she could get competitive over the weirdest stuff.

My father got four pairs of XL gray sweatpants under the tree that year. My father was not an extra large man...................

Two teeny bopper cashiers were standing under the red light with their price guns at the ready. Ready to mark the Fruit of the Loom down to a mere dollar. By the time the crowd of women calmed down.................those two little pimply faced girls were shaking.

I loved this stuff! You know you would have too!

The red light special lamp was on wheels. The three of us watched it being wheeled towards the toy section. I was the youngest in the family. There were no grandchildren yet. These women should have lost interest when the red light went towards the toys.

But, no!

"Good evening shoppers! Santa needs a little help this year! Do you know a little girl that would love to find an exclusive 1973 Deluxe Bride Doll under the tree? We know you do!" said the announcement as the red light started swirling and making it's siren noise.

My mother, Rose and the shopping cart barrelled towards the toy section.

"Ma! Rose! You do not have any little girls on your list! Do you just like being in the middle of a riot?" I called after them.

I guess they did.

I stood back as a crowd of women terrorized the same two sales associates holding pricing guns.

Mom and Rose both came out of the heap holding one bride doll apiece.

The gorgeous dolls were marked down to $3.00 a piece. I remembered back to other trips to stores like this when I was a tiny little girl. How many times did I beg for a bride doll? How many times did I get turned down?

My mother looked up at me. The frenzy left her eyes.

"What in the hell are we going to do with these dolls?" she asked Rose.

"I don't know!" yelled Rose. "I just ran and grabbed one because you did!"

I took the dolls out of their hands and put them on the bottom of the cart.

"I'll pay for those." I said. "The Marines are collecting toys outside. I really, really liked the looks of those Marines. Maybe that's what I'll ask Santa for this year."

"A doll?" my mother asked.

"Jesus, Ellie! Darlene doesn't want a doll. She wants herself a Marine!" crowed Rose with a big grin on her face.

"Oh, dear God." whispered my mother.

You see why I loved shopping with these two?

I glanced at my watch.

"Mom. Food. Now. Feed me. Grilled cheese. Tomato soup. Pepsi. Now. Over there! There's a table free. And, our date is waiting." I said as I pushed the two women over to the luncheonette railing. I parked the cart and greeted the store detective.

Mom and Rose glared at me. I had invited their nemesis to eat with us? The woman that had been following them around for ten years? This woman had been skulking behind displays for so many years................my mother knew the squeak of her sneakers.

The four of us ordered and ate and surprisingly.............had a great old time.

"All these years...........I have never ever thought you were thieves. I'm sorry I made you uncomfortable. But, I miss my sisters. I have four of them.............and you two are just so much fun! The way you argue and put things back.

And, fight over something when it's the last one. I guess I just wanted to be shopping with you. And, then? Your daughter invites me to eat with you! This is great! Dinner is on me." the store detective said.

We ate and then gave the store detective a hug and said "See you next year!"

We went to check out. Rose paid for her stuff and had a dollar to spare. My mother loaded up the counter. She was two dollars short. She stiffened up and breathed funny.

"Oh, my God! I'm going to have to use my charge card! Your poor father. He's going to self combust! This is totally going to ruin his Christmas." she whispered to me.

I opened my purse and handed her the money she needed.

"You have money? Why didn't you do any Christmas shopping then?" she asked me.

"I shop alone." I replied.

I paid for the two beautiful bride dolls. We headed out the door.

"You ladies load up the car while I go and talk with the Marines." I said as I walked away.

Both of those young Marines were very nice by the way. They both asked for my phone number. They both lost interest as soon as I told them my Daddy used to be a Marine. WWII. Drill Sergeant.

"Darlene! You are sixteen years old. Do not bring home a Marine for Christmas!" my mother said loud enough for the boys in uniform to hear.

What a wing man. Thanks Ma!

"Ellie!" Rose hissed. "Get in the car! Darlene likes to shop alone!"

****

Christmas Snow On Columbus Street

I'm a social person. I like company. But, I also need quiet. I can be entertaining at a party. But, I am just as glad to get home and give my ears and voice a rest.

The college years were wonderful in so many ways. Best of all was my roommate. We clicked. We got each other. We talked into the night. She needed lots of quiet to do her studying. That was fine by me.

I was a Journalism Major. So, I had a lot of writing to do. Writing comes easy to me. But, the brain has to be engaged to come up with coherent thoughts on the page. I needed quiet too.

Christmas break was welcome. My roommate and I exchanged small gifts. We cleaned up the dorm room. We washed any dirty dishes and cleaned out our small refrigerator. We waited for our Dads to come and break us out of the dormitory. We hugged and said goodbye knowing that we needed a break from each other's faces and voices.

I went home for Christmas and found two parents that had missed me badly. They brewed tea and warmed their hands on the cups. They just stared at me over the little maple kitchen table.

Then they questioned me.

Did I do well in classes? Was my roommate a nice girl or was she "wise"? Did I meet any nice boys? Did I walk around New Haven all by myself after dark? Did I know enough to stay safe? My face looked thin. Had I been eating? On the other hand............my backside looked fuller. Had I eaten too many desserts in the cafeteria? When was the last time I had eaten a vegetable?

"Life isn't all butterscotch pudding." my mother quoted at me.

I sighed and knew it was going to be a noisy long month.

I got on the phone and called my old boss at KFC. He needed my help and put me on the schedule for 30 hours a week throughout the month of December.

I worked. I slept. I read books. I went Christmas shopping. I did most of it all by myself.

I needed quiet.

My mother thought I was withdrawn. That meant I must be troubled by something. She questioned me every time I got within earshot. She could find nothing wrong with me. Except that I kept disappearing up the wooden stairs to my cold bedroom. The heat never really reached my room.

I liked it that way. I had found my dorm room to be stifling hot.

My father perhaps knew me best of all.

"Let her be, Ellie. There is nothing wrong with our Little Girl. She's been forced to share a room. She's been surrounded by noisy females looking for company and someone to go to dinner with. She sits in lecture halls with hundreds of people. She couldn't find quiet. She's always needed a lot of alone time. Just let her be." he told her.

She left me alone with my quiet thoughts for a few days.

My father smiled knowingly when I put the radio on and sang along while I baked his favorite cookies. He grinned when I egged my mother into singing the Hallelujah Chorus with me. She didn't know it so she made up the words.

I walked to work even though my father offered me his second car. My mother was right about the butterscotch pudding at school. Walking both ways every day eventually loosened up my pants.

Christmas Eve was coming. My mother tore through the house dusting and shining and vacuuming. I stayed out of her way. Her eyes would narrow and I'd get asked if I was a princess. A queen perhaps.

"Perhaps Her Highness would deem fit to take this Lemon Pledge and shine up the woodwork for our Christmas company." she said as she shoved a dust rag into my hand.

"And, then, perhaps Princess Darlene might go on upstairs and make that bed. And, pick up those dirty clothes. Does royalty know how to run a washing machine? " she asked in her snootiest voice.

I was over my need for quiet and self reflection. I dusted but I put my royal foot down to doing my own laundry. What was this woman thinking?

"Tell you what, Ma. You know those fancy Christmas cookies that only I know how to bake? I'll trade you five dozen cookies for two loads of clean laundry." I bartered.

"It's a deal." she replied. "Get baking."

I worked at KFC until 4 pm on Christmas Eve. I walked home through the quiet streets. It was getting dark and the colorful Christmas lights glowed in the bushes of my neighbor's yards. Picture windows were full of beautiful lighted Christmas trees. Shades weren't drawn against the darkness.

The noise of families gathered in dining rooms and living rooms spilled out windows cracked against the heat of too many people gathered in too small rooms.

I stopped on the sidewalk and looked at the little Cape Cod house on Columbus Street that was my home. Inside I saw my mother busy in the kitchen. My father was getting a fire going in his fireplace. Just for looks. The downstairs was cozy without it's help.

The snowflakes that fell were big. The fluffy kind. The ones that look like mini versions of the paper snowflakes we'd cut out of folded paper in grammar school. The kind of snowflakes that make a shushing noise as they rush past your ears. The kind that make you throw your head back and close your eyes. You want to feel their weight on your eyelashes. You want to taste them on your tongue.

The kind of snowflakes that make a noise like quiet.

I was completely happy in that moment. Looking at my home on Columbus Street. I could see my parents through the windows. The mother that worried about me. The father that understood me.

I smiled when I thought of my first report card from college that had come in the mail. I had passed everything and had earned A's in all my writing classes. There had even been a handwritten note from my Creative Writing teacher. She told me that she had never come across "one so young that had already found her voice."

When I'm completely happy............I sing. I stood in that little front yard all alone. And, I sang.

"Let there be peace on earth and let it begin with me." I sang from my old Round Table Singer days. I sang the whole thing. My parents listened from behind the Christmas tree in the picture window. My father held my mother back. I know she must have wanted to throw open that front door to ask me if I had completely lost it.

I took a snapshot in my head. My heart was full. I was fully recuperated from my first semester away from home. I had survived. I had excelled in everything I thought was important. And, I was home again. For Christmas.

I must remember this moment I thought. Just as it is. I was wise enough at age 18 to know that these kinds of moments are scarce. A person is lucky to have a moment such as this. It must be remembered.

I finished the song and the quiet of the snow took over Columbus Street once again.

I hadn't noticed the neighbor man across the street gathering firewood at the top of his driveway. He had stood completely still while I had performed my song for the falling snow. For Christmas.

"Merry Christmas, Darlene." he said quietly from his driveway with his arms full of wood.

"That was something I'll never ever forget. Ever." he almost whispered to me from across the street.

But, I heard him.

The snow was that quiet.

****

Getting To Know You Christmas

I got engaged when I was nineteen years old. I had never bothered dating. I had never been able to stand a boy for more than two weeks. I don't think my husband of forty years realizes how he sneaked in under my "Don't need a man" radar.

I met Michael in August. His sister was about to marry my brother. I ignored him throughout August and most of September. One day he was making me roll my eyes with his attentions. The next minute I was smitten.

The engagement ring landed on my finger in November. I was still living in a dormitory at college. Michael was working full time and living in a little efficiency apartment on his own.

He did a lot of driving in his little white Ford Gremlin. It was a triangle that he drove. New London to New Haven to pick me up from school. On to Manchester to take me home to my parents for a weekend.

Over and over again.

He looked forward to our wedding coming up in August for obvious reasons. But, I think he was also tired of driving. He was sick of pumping gas into that strange little car.

He picked me up from college and drove me home for my month long Christmas break. I chatted away in the car for the hour and a half ride. He did a lot of blinking. He was quiet. I think he was very tired.

We arrived at my parent's house. We would spend the night there and then go to his parent's house for the weekend. His apartment was close to them. I got to spend a lot of time with him in his town. His parents didn't seem to watch us like hawks like mine did.

My mother fussed over us. My father clapped Michael on the back and handed him a beer. We all sat down for early afternoon snacks at the little kitchen table decorated with plastic Santa place mats.

My parents were full of chat. They hadn't seen me in weeks. They were trying to get to know their future son-in-law in the few hours that I allotted them every now and then.

Michael wasn't responding much. And, when he did? His responses were strange and the thoughts were half finished.

My father recognized what he was seeing.

"So, young Mike! How many days have you worked in a row without a day off?" Daddy asked him.

Michael thought about it as he finished off the can of beer.

"By my count? 22 days without a day off, sir. Darlene's been writing for her end of the year papers. She's been studying for exams. I figured if I couldn't see her.........I might as well work. Honeymoons don't pay for themselves." he said.

I looked at my fiance. 22 days at work. No time off. On purpose. He was serious about providing for me. Oh, this poor soul with his eyes at half mast. I should have driven home. I hadn't realized how very tired he really was.

"Why don't you go upstairs and have a nap?" my mother suggested.

"I'm a grown man." Michael replied. "I don't take naps. What am I? A baby?" he snipped at my mother.

I stood up and pushed my chair gently under the table.

"Michael? Upstairs. Now, please." I said in a quiet voice. It was early days but I already knew that this was a man that didn't like to be told what to do.

Michael was a little confused. What couldn't be said in front of my parents? He already knew that I was a Mommy or Daddy's girl. Depended which day of the week it was.

He hauled himself up the wooden stairs. I was behind him. I was holding onto his hips and giving him a push up the treads. I got to the top of the stairs. I took him by the shoulders and aimed him to the left.

My bedroom was glowing for Christmas. My mother had shined the paneled walls. They glowed and smelled of Murphy's Oil Soap. The wooden floors that I had helped Daddy lay when I was a tiny little girl were slippery with wax. The white sheer crisscrossed curtains at the windows were white and newly starched.

A little Christmas tree glowed from the top of my empty desk. My gold angora cat snored and purred from the bottom of the bed. She looked like a Christmas postcard against the red and green of the holiday quilt that covered my brass bed.

The exhausted man that was my fiance looked around the room with blurry eyes.

"Is this real?" he asked me.

"Yes, it's real." I answered.

I pulled the covers back from the bed. I sat Michael down on the edge of the bed. I bent down and removed his shoes and socks. I pushed him back and covered him up with the sweet Downy scent of the sheets and quilt.

"Why'd you take my socks off?" he said in a half asleep whisper.

"My mother has buffed and waxed the floors up here for Christmas. Do not walk around here wearing just socks. You'll break your neck. Barefoot or shoes are fine." I said as I sat at the edge of the bed.

"I don't take naps." he said with a huge break the hinges yawn.

"You do today." I answered.

"I don't think I like cats that much. I don't know that I want a cat sleeping with me." he said as he punched the pillow into the shape that he liked.

'Oh, that's not up to you, honey. If she likes the smell of you? She'll stay and purr you to sleep. No better feeling." I said in a flat monotone voice.

I was talking a man that does not nap into taking a nap.

"Don't let me sleep too long!" he said and almost sat up.

"No. I'll let you sleep for two hours." I said in my soothing go to sleep voice. "When you wake up you can have a nice beef stew that my mother will make. You can talk and drink another beer with my Daddy. I'm going to go down and make you a nice apple pie. After dinner we'll play cards. And, then we'll watch a Christmas movie on

TV if you can't sleep. Tomorrow we'll go to your house. We're going to buy a Christmas tree. And, we'll go to the department store and buy some ornaments. We'll have dinner with your parents. It will be such a great weekend. So, go to sleep now." I said as I stood up from the bed.

I stood up to sneak out of the room. I thought I had talked him to sleep.

I was almost to the door when I heard his voice again.

"You know how to make pies?" he asked.

"Yes. I do. I'm very good at it." I replied.

"Why, didn't I know this? How many different kinds of pies do you know how to make?" he asked as my cat curled up under his chin.

"Two." I said as I inched my way towards the head of the stairs.

"Apple and Strawberry Rhubarb?" he wanted to know.

"No. With or without tops." I said with one foot on the stairs.

"She knows how to make pies!" Michael told the cat. "Did you know that?"

I came down the stairs. My father sat on the couch reading a newspaper. My mother flitted around the room trying to cover up that she had been listening from the bottom rung.

"Boy, he gets a little crabby when he's overtired." my mother said in a semi accusatory way.

"I wouldn't know, Ma. I don't live with the man." I said as I shooed her out of my way.

My father chuckled.

"He's not doing half bad for a guy that hasn't taken a day off in three weeks. I'd hire him." said my Daddy; the engineering supervisor.

"I just promised him an apple pie." I told my mother. "Do I need to go to the store?"

"No, we have apples and everything you need for your pie crust. How did you know I was going to make beef stew tonight?" she asked me with her head tilted to the side.

"You always make me beef stew when I come home from school." I replied.

My father chuckled again from the couch.

My mother took the counter. I used the kitchen table to roll out the dough. She used the oven burners. I used the oven. An hour later the smells coming from the kitchen were pretty spectacular.

My father came around the corner. He said "Hey, Little Girl! I found a radio station that you'll like. Nothing but Christmas music from now until New Years!" He put the radio in the den on low volume.

I was up to my elbows in sudsy water in the sink. I sang along to the Hallelujah Chorus. I had found enough time this semester to sing with the college chorus. We had sung Handel's masterpiece with the New Haven Symphony Orchestra the week before.

I turned to find Michael standing in the hallway. He looked around like he was still half asleep. He looked a little stunned.

"I woke up in the most beautiful room. There was a Christmas tree in the corner. A beautiful gold cat was purring on my chest. I smelled wonderful things. Beef stew. And, apple pie. I love apple pie. I dreamed that Darlene knew how to bake. I mean she's a nineteen year old girl. She doesn't really know how to bake does she?' he asked no one in particular.

My father grinned from the table. This was a man that knew how it was to be this tired. My mother giggled at him from the stove wearing pot holders on each hand.

Michael continued. "And, then.............I heard the most beautiful music. And, this voice! This voice was coming from the kitchen. The most beautiful voice!"

Michael looked at me in awe.

"Do you sing?" he asked me.

****

The Tribe At Christmas

There was a beautiful photo of my maternal grandmother on my parent's bedroom wall. I had never met her as she died before I was born. Her hair was soft and brown and wrapped around her face in a braid. She had bright friendly eyes and very high cheek bones.

I'd look at her photo while I helped my mother fold towels on the bed. She'd look up at the photo too and remember and share stories of my grandmother. I thought the woman in the photo looked a lot more fun than the one my mother described.

She described the woman who fought to feed her family during the Depression. Those were the "God Will Provide" stories. This photo showed me the fun one that liked to sing around the piano at night.

"Your grandmother was half French Canadian and half Indian, Darlene." I know the politically correct term now is Native American, but my mother used the term Indian. So, I will too.

"Her mother was an Indian princess. So, you are part Indian princess too."

I don't think my mother was trying to embellish by calling her a princess. I don't think she was trying to Disney her story up. I think she was just repeating what she'd been told herself.

"But, I can't remember what tribe she was from. I never can. Next time I see my brother Jimmy I will ask him again. I have got to write it down." she said as she stacked the towels.

It wasn't long before Uncle Jimmy came for a visit. I noticed he shared the same high cheek bones his mother had. I asked him the name of the tribe.

He said "I don't know why your mother can never remember it. She asks me over and over. It was the Nipmuc tribe. The Nipmucs of Massachusetts." he answered.

My mom wrote it down on a slip of paper. Perhaps she knew she'd eventually mislay it. I could see her lips moving as she mumbled. She was playing the word association game with herself. She was coming up with a word that sounded close as a reminder. I wondered what word she could possibly come up with that would rhyme with or almost sound like Nipmuc. I forgot to ask.

Years later my fiance; Michael was sitting in my mother's kitchen for his first Anderson Christmas. The house was small and it was full. A few were in the living room trying to get the 8 mm projector working. There was some swearing and some laughing going on.

Someone upstairs dropped something over our heads with a big bang. I was leaning through the hatch into the kitchen and loudly telling anyone that could hear me that "It's A Wonderful Life" was about to begin on TV. Someone in the bathroom was yelling "Is there any more toilet paper? Can anyone hear me? Dear, God! I need some toilet paper!"

My mother was talking with Michael as he snacked at the kitchen table. She never stopped talking as she went to the linen closet in the hallway. She grabbed a roll of toilet paper, opened the bathroom door a crack and threw it at someone's head. She didn't know who and they didn't want her to know.

There was a lot of whooping coming from the basement where the men were drinking beer and having a billiards tournament. Michael was taking a break from them as he was waiting to play the winner.

There were lots of loud people doing lots of things while a Christmas tree blinked in the corner. Michael wasn't quite used to this much noise and movement during a holiday. So, he was kind of sitting in the corner blinking himself.

"Did you know Darlene is part Indian, Michael?" my mother asked. "Her great grandmother was an Indian princess. Now, what was the name of the tribe?" she pondered.

My mother started moving her lips as she tried to remember her word association game.

I leaned through the hatch and asked my mother for the bag of Hershey Kisses sitting on the counter. She threw them to me missing Michael's ear by an inch as she came up with the answer. Well, she almost came up with the answer.

"We are Nitwits, Michael. Can you believe it? We are part of the Nitwit Tribe." she proudly exclaimed.

Michael tried valiantly to keep a straight face as he replied, "Yes, Mrs. Anderson. I really can believe that you're all part of the Nitwit Tribe."

"Welcome to the Nitwits, Michael! You're one of us now!" replied my mother.

****

Windows Aglow

Pretty decorations in a store window entices customers to come in. It's especially important in small stores without a big corporation of advertisers behind them.

I've spent a lot of happy hours decorating store windows.

I was a newlywed and got a full time cashier job at a pharmacy down the street. It was a good job in that it was walking distance. We only owned one car at the time.

This pharmacy had been in the same spot forever. How could I tell? It looked like a general store from Little House in the Prairie in there. The long thin store had built in shelving that lined the walls. They were made out of wood. Drawers were fit under the shelving.

The store itself was a priceless antique.

I rang people up on a huge antique cash register. It was 1978 and the owner didn't think it was weird that he owned a cash register that had a hand crank on the side. Children loved to buy their candy at this store because they loved the ca-ching of that machine.

The store was failing.

The owner was the pharmacist. I'm sure he was a dedicated pill counter. He took great pride in knowing all of his customers. He took time to explain their medications to the people.

But, a businessman he was not.

He waved away driver's licenses when people paid by check. He would send me to a corner market to buy bread and milk and a package of cookies. He'd deliver medication to an old lady himself. He brought her groceries and never charged her.

He hired me the day I asked for a job. Because, he said "I like the looks of you. I have a good feeling about you! You can start right now."

I already knew how to run a cash register. Even if I had to turn a crank to do so. I priced items for sale and I went to put them on the shelves. Sticky dirty rotten shelves. Oh, they were antique wooden shelves but they were unloved. They were filthy.

I had been working for Mr. Able for three hours. I stood in front of him at the prescription counter and I just waited. He was counting pills and I didn't want him to lose count.

He looked up and smiled.

"What can I do for you Diane?" he asked.

"My name is Darlene." I responded. "I would like to go to the corner market and buy some Murphy's Oil Soap. I'll be back in five minutes. I have to start washing these shelves before I restock them. Do you know what you have here? These original wooden fixtures were made by a carpenter. People should shop here just for the old fashioned experience." I said to him.

He blinked at me. Like an owl.

No, he didn't know what he had here. This man that still rang out people on hand cranked cash registers.

"Sure!" he said. "Go to the store and buy whatever you need. You're going to clean? And, no one asked you to? I like your initiative, Little Lady." He pushed a deep No Sale button on the register and handed me some money.

"I'll bring you back the receipt." I said.

"No need, I trust you." he said to me. A young woman he had known for three hours.

Mr. Able had a crowded back room the size of a small sewing room. It included an overheated stall sized bathroom. That bathroom was always 100 degrees because the radiator in there ran the full length of the tiny room.

The back room also housed a Bob Cratchit desk complete with full time ancient female accountant sitting in a rocking leather chair.

I have no idea why he needed this full time person. My guess? Is that he felt sorry for her. He kept her gainfully employed for forty hours a week. Her job could have been done from home in three hours a month.

Like I said. He was no businessman.

This woman took an instant dislike to me. I had youth. I had energy. Her full time job became rolling her eyes at me. Pointing to her watch when she thought I was two minutes late in the morning.

I couldn't be bothered to interact with her. I couldn't be bothered to tell her that her watch was always set ten minutes ahead.

I would sing quietly to myself when the store was empty. The witch in the back room would complain about this to Mr. Able. He would laugh and yell out from behind the prescription counter.

"If that's the Hallelujah Chorus you're singing, Darlene! Louder! Turn up your volume! Make an old man happy!" he'd say.

So, I scrubbed and I cleaned and I sang. I emptied out a dirty glass case full of expensive perfumes. Perfumes that no one would buy because they were covered in dust. I poked around in drawers and cupboards. I found a cubbie that some long dead window decorator had stored their stuff in.

I shook the dust off of bolts of satin fabric. I lined the glass cabinets with green and red satin. Glass Santas. Crystal snowmen. Elves that were older than I was. All of this was in that forgotten cupboard. I put back the rows of perfumes. I repriced things. The prices went up. I put in a little sign that said "The antique Christmas ornaments are not for sale."

Next, I went to work on the glorious wooden shelves full of wine bottles. Yes, this little pharmacy also had a liquor license. I dusted bottles. I knew nothing about wine but I tried to categorize what I was seeing.

There was a little old man that worked across the street. Every day he came in and bought a small bottle of brandy. He owned a little shoe repair business. He looked like a tiny old elf. He was very sweet. I thought he was about a hundred years old. But, that was just because I was so young.

I had uncovered a lot of red wine that looked old to me. "Red wine gets better with age?" I asked the little gnome man.

"Oh, my God!" he said as he perused the bottles I had been cleaning up.

"This is a gold mine!" he declared. "Able! Get over here! Call the liquor store on the corner. Have them come and look at this stuff! You can pay the rent for two months just by selling these ten bottles."

"I don't pay rent! I own this building." said Mr. Able. He tried to wave off the old man with the knowledge of wine.

Like I said. He was no businessman.

"Then pay your freaking taxes with the money, man! I'll do it for you. Girlie! Put those bottles on the floor where no one can see them. I'll have the guy in here to give you a price within the hour!" he said as he mumbled his way out the door.

Mr. Able sold ten bottles of wine an hour later. He looked kind of shocked. He tried to press a hundred dollars into my hand.

I turned him down. I asked him to order more perfume for the case instead.

Mr. Able looked at me and smiled. "You're some man's daughter. I never had a daughter. I have two ungrateful sons. Your father is such a lucky man." he said as he went back to counting pills.

The witch left for the day. As she walked by me she said "Don't you think you're something special."

I left an hour later. I was dirty and covered with cob webs. But, I think I had made a difference. Even, at that young age............I thought that was important.

I stood in front of the store and smiled. I worked here now. I was helpful and it was appreciated.

I looked at the two storefront windows with the ancient curved glass. The glass was filthy. The right hand window showcased a metal walker. The left hand window actually held a dust covered portable potty for the bedridden.

Oh, my God!

I would do something about that tomorrow.

Christmas was coming. The female in me protested at the state of those windows. The dust and dirt and grime had to go. So did the hospital equipment. This might be a drug store. But, I knew there were boxes of chocolates for sale. Perfume and beautiful makeup kits that I had just ordered. Wine. Brandy. Books.................I would have to go through those books and make sure Mr. Able wasn't selling first editions for fifty cents.

The next day I started cleaning the windows after the newspaper buying crowd was gone. I uncovered parquet floors under the layers of grime. I grabbed a few copies of old newspapers and made the windows shine.

Customers came in while I was cleaning. Mr. Able came to my rescue. He spoke to the silent dusty accountant in the back room.

"Helen!" he barked. "Get on that cash register so Darlene can clean those windows. You can still walk can't you? Get a move on woman! Christmas is coming and we've got to decorate!" he said as he started to sing Jingle Bells at the top of his lungs.

So, her name was Helen. Helen gave me dirty looks but she obviously knew how to crank that cash register.

I stood outside on the sidewalk. The last of the autumn leaves skittered by me on the sidewalk. I hugged my shoulders from the cold. I stared at the empty clean windows and I planned.

I went to the school supply section. I grabbed a box of poster paint. I went to the cleaning supply aisle and took a bottle of dish soap. I found some empty plastic containers in the back room. I mixed up some soapy paint. I had heard somewhere that this was the way to paint on glass.

I decorated the window edges like they were stained glass. The sun was setting early at that time of year. I finished and went outside to see. Yes! The light glowing from the inside of the store indeed made the windows look like ancient stained glass.

My husband dropped me off at work the next morning. He helped me unload the car. I had many empty boxes wrapped like Christmas gifts. I had a small artificial tree. Lights. Ornaments. Strings of wooden beads that looked like cranberries. A pewter lamp that had a stained glass shade.

First thing first. I went to the back room and stared down the unfriendly accountant. She glared back.

"I need your chair." I said.

"Whaaaaaat?" she asked.

I pushed a regular desk chair on wheels towards her.

"I need that leather chair you're sitting in for the front window display. It is antique. It is real leather. I'm going to clean it up and put it in the front window. " I explained.

"Over my dead body, little Miss Aren't You The Favorite." she answered in a hiss.

"Over your dead body?" I asked. "Well, if I have to. If you force me to. You and I both know that a monkey with a calculator could do your job in three hours a month. Do I have to do it over your dead body? Or, do you want to switch chairs for a month?" I asked.

She got up and pushed the leather chair at me. It banged me in the shins. Those bruises only lasted a week.

"Oh, and I'll need that little mahogany book case there in the corner. You can stack your receipts from 1960 on the floor until the holidays are over." I said. She ignored me. I was no longer there. My voice could no longer be heard.

So, I just took the little bookcase.

I put up tension curtain rods. I thread old fashioned lace like curtains from home onto them. I put one in each of the windows. I tied the curtains back to frame the windows.

I set the scene. The cleaned up leather chair sat in a window with a Christmas throw blanket on it inviting the passerby to sit on down. A little table sat next to the chair. The lamp glowed from the tabletop. A box of chocolates were open and a few pieces were missing. Pill bottles also littered the table top.

This was a pharmacy after all.

The other window had the decorated and lit up Christmas tree. The book shelf stood behind it. I'd found plenty of books to make the book shelf look lived in. Presents and teddy bears and dolls spilled out from under the tree. A glass tray from home presented a bottle of wine and a crystal wine glass.

This was a pharmacy that had a stock of hundreds of bottles of wine after all.

I was tired. I was dirty. Helen wasn't happy ringing out customers. I had forgotten to take my half an hour lunch break

I invited Mr. Able to come out onto the sidewalk just as dusk was upon us.

The windows glowed from within. The stained glass effect was beautiful and nostalgic. The two scenes were cozy and inviting. Mr. Able got misty eyed. He sniffed.

"My mother……………back in the old days………….she was the one that did the windows. The left one………………she'd do in blues and purples and there would be a menorah. The right was all Santa Claus and snow and made the little kiddies happy. I have to say though. You're twice the artist she was. You paint a story with the furnishings. It's like someone has just stepped away for a minute. They'll be right back. Thank you." he said.

He continued.

"Thank you for doing much more than I pay you do. Thank you for taking the initiative. Thank you for smiling.

Thank you for telling your stories. Thank you for singing."
he said as he went back inside.

I shook the dirt out of the WELCOME mat and followed
him back inside.

I arrived the next morning for work. I looked at the
glowing windows with pride. I noticed a small menorah
had been added to the table on the left.

It was perfect.

The next day a lady in a suit visited. She was carrying a
clip board. She visited with Mr. Able in the back of the
store for a while.

Mr. Able yelled to me from the back. "Darlene. Pay this
woman twenty five dollars from the till. It's my dues for
The Downtown Business Association. Put a note in the
drawer."

I gave the woman the money and put the note in the
drawer.

A few days later the woman was back visiting with Mr.
Able again. He was back there chatting away. He was
laughing and having a good time.

The end of my day approached. I finished pulling the old
magazines and replaced them with the new. I restocked

the candy aisle. I dusted the liquor section. I hummed along to the Christmas music on the radio.

Mr. Able stood in front of me.

"I joined the Downtown Business Association again for a reason." he said to me.

Okay? I thought to myself.

"There is a yearly contest. A contest for Best Front Christmas Windows. The woman that visited a few days ago thought we had a chance of winning. She told me that we'd only be in the running if I paid my dues. So, I did." he said.

And? I asked myself.

"She said that the whole downtown is talking. They couldn't believe that the dusty walker and potty were finally gone from my store front. They figured that I had finally moved past my mother being gone. You know. Since she was the one that did the windows all those years ago. So." he said as he rocked on his feet.

His shoes squeaked.

"You won!" he said as he handed me an envelope.

I looked in the envelope and saw a crisp fifty dollar bill.

My eyes flew open. I'd never seen a fifty dollar bill before.

"Thank you for the beautiful windows." he said.

"But, mostly? Thank you for singing."

"My mother……………she……………was a singer."

****

The Christmas Contest

Christmas was over. Except for the burping. The huge meal had been eaten. The dishwasher chugged away in the kitchen. The trash cans were full of wrapping paper. The cat snored on the couch. Dessert had been waved away by a houseful of adults that could no longer button their pants.

"One hour nap!" I declared. "And, then we play games!"

I'm not a very competitive soul. But, I do like to play games. Like charades. Cranium. Trivial Pursuit. Poker for a nickle a chip. I have no need to win. It's just a lot of fun playing games with my kids now that they're adults.

Like I said…………I'm not competitive. But, everyone else in this house? Wow! They grow fangs. They like to win. They like to crow. They call do-over! They actually read the rules on the inside of the box outloud to no one listening when they are at a disadvantage.

My dear daughter even dumped me as her partner in the middle of a game once. She announced that we had the same strengths and the same weaknesses. So we weren't fit partners. This was right after I did a great impression of Ed McMahon. Everyone else around the table were biting their lips to keep themselves from calling out his name to the other team. But, my daughter? I guess she just didn't know who he was.

She dumped me anyway. Oh, don't feel sorry for me. That night gave me a life long "The Night You Were Mean To Me" story. I can get a lot of mileage out it.

I was a newlywed at age 20. I flitted around our new apartment for a few months. I made curtains. I rearranged furniture so that my new husband could come home at midnight and trip over chairs.

He finally told me it was time to get a job.

So, I did.

I interviewed for a twenty hour cashier job at a big drug store. It was like a CVS but without a druggist. I have no idea why Drug was in the name of the store when there was no prescription counter.

Six weeks later I was the manager because of people quitting or moving away. The district manager said "Oh, you'll be just fine. I live in town. I'll drop in all the time. No worries."

It's a good thing I'm a fast learner. I hardly ever saw the guy.

Until he made me hire his sixteen year old daughter at Christmas time.

I interviewed the girl. Please, don't get mad at me. But…………………she was as dumb as a box of rocks. At twenty years of age……………I actually had the audacity to tell her father………the district manager…………my boss…………that his daughter just wasn't a good fit. She doesn't know how to count. She rolled her eyes at me. She wore a tee shirt to an interview……….her belly button had winked at me.

She also said "Like…………like……………duh!" to me during that interview.

He said "You're hiring her anyways." as he walked out the door.

Christmas was coming. The truck was leaving me lots and lots of stuff for a seasonal aisle. I was given maps on how to merchandise that aisle. I had more toys than I had room for in the toy aisle.

I called the district manager and asked "Who ordered all this stuff?" It was a good question. Because, you see.............as manager I did the ordering.

"I did." he said. "Pretend you work at the North Pole. Get that stuff out there. Sell. Sell. Sell!"

Then he hung up on me.

I called him back.

"I need more hours. Not for me...........but for the four part timers. Including your daughter. Who still can't count by the way. Double their hours and I'll sell all this extra stuff." I said.

I had him at "She still can't count."

"Done! Oh, and decorate those windows for Christmas. Take whatever you need from the store to do it. Put whatever you use on form 1XLT (Huh?). Northpole! Santa! Elves! I want to see it snowing in there, damn it!" he yelled over the phone line.

Then he hung up on me again.

I ran this store with a full time assistant manager. She was an absolute sweetheart. She loved me. She worked hard and did extra. But, she was always tired. She was a newlywed too. And, well, what's a nice way to put this.

She was always tired because she and her new husband were always going at it like bunny rabbits.

It got to the point I wouldn't allow him in the store…………….they were always sneaking off into dark corners of the back room. Yeah, I'm not kidding.

I had four teenagers from the local high school working part time. I hadn't hired any of them. They were just sort of thrown in my lap.

One was a cheerleader and she was forever asking for days off for sporting events. One was a pretty girl that dressed like a hippie and she was almost mute. She was that shy. One was a Goth before there were Goths. She had long color infused hair and black lipstick. She was an artist.

And, then there was the boss's daughter. A big smile on her face. Willing but not able. Her drawer came up twenty bucks short or over every shift.

The phone rang. It was the boss again. "Oh, by the way. The reason I want those windows decorated. The reason I want those extra displays highlighted………….I've entered the store in the nationwide decorating contest. Take photos of it all in two weeks. Send it to the national office." he said.

A contest? Oh, dear God. As if I didn't have enough to deal with. The day before a water main had broken in the parking lot. It had been like Niagra Falls out there for most of the day. Though, I admit. The firemen were nice to look at.

"And, Sweetheart!" ....yes, bosses were allowed to call you Sweetheart way back then............"Don't get your hopes up. Small stores like yours never ever......let me repeat this.............never ever win. I had to have at least one entry. All the other managers told me to take a hike. So, you're it Sweetheart!" he said as he banged the phone down.

I sat down in my little office. I put my head in my hands. I took out the schedules I had made for the next two weeks. I ripped them up. I redid them adding the extra hours. I called all the girls in for a meeting.

They all ignored each other. They belonged to different cliques in high school. I realized Goth didn't mix with Fake Hippie didn't mix with Cheerleader. But, really. I didn't have time for that crap.

That's what I told them. They got it. I took them on a tour. I showed them the big empty windows. I had them envision where extra displays of children's books were going to go. Eight feet of dolls. Aisles of candy and wrapping paper.

"You're on the clock, right now. For two hours. Go in the back room and make a plan. Shelving. Paint. Wrapping paper. Whatever you need. Pile it up so I can write it down. This is a contest. I have no idea what the prize is yet. I've been told we can't possibly win. You know what, girls? That pisses me off. Why can't you win? Put your differences aside and figure out what you want to do. I'll run the store." I told them and I shooed them into the back room.

They came up with a plan. The windows were going to depict Santa's Workshop. I was handed drawings by the Goth Girl. They were rudimentary but that girl had talent. The books were going to be sold by a full sized Big Bird like character made out of tissue paper. A Cookie Monster like creature was going to rule over the candy aisle. Wrapped gifts were going to hang from the high ceilings by wires.

I'm not competitive. But, these girls sure were.

"I don't do ladders." I whispered out loud.

"I do!" said my assistant manager's husband. He had somehow sneaked into the building without me noticing.

"Clouds! And, stars! I'm great at painting clouds and stars!" said the assistant manager.

They were all in and they didn't even know what the prize was.

I put the whole gang on together two full Saturdays in a row. They worked well together. I heard lots of laughing and singing while they worked. They painted and decorated while I took care of customers and filled the shelves with deodorant and shampoo.

I even overheard the Goth Girl say to the boss's daughter "You just think you can't count. It's like a mind block. I can teach you how to make change in an hour I bet. No biggie. Don't let anyone including your father tell you that you can't count. After school on Monday. Parking lot. I'll teach you."

I had no more hours to give them. They weren't entirely done with their creations. They got together and talked about it. They came and told me that they were all coming in on Sunday at noon. For free. To finish their artwork.

I promised them lunch. That's the least I could do. Now, I had to figure out how I was going to pay for pizza and salads for this crew.

They worked that Sunday all the way until it was closing time. Darkness fell over the parking lot. We all spilled out the door. That group of teenage girls became quiet as they looked at the beautiful Victorian Santa's Workshop that had taken over our plain glass windows.

I took photos. Their artwork was glorious! I took photos of the windows. I took photos of them in front of the windows. Blowing kisses at Santa. Patting elves on the head. They were having a blast.

They were friends.

I sent off the photos to the national headquarters. I included a letter.

It went something like..............

"I manage a small store in Ct. We don't have the square footage that a lot of city stores have. But, we are important to this town. I have no idea why this contest was invented. But, I have to thank you. Four girls that had nothing in common became friends while decorating this store. They've exchanged phone numbers. They go to the movies together now. This contest gave them a common goal. It doesn't matter if they win the prize or not. They are already winners. Because? Now, they are friends. Merry Christmas."

The district manager paid me a visit a week later.

I put everyone together on the schedule for one last time. I threw a little Christmas party in that big dark cave of a back room. All the food and drink came from the store with the boss's permission

The girls were all laughing and having fun. They exchanged little gifts. They made plans for their school break.

I interrupted them..

"Well, ladies. You are artists! Sales are up 15%. That's nothing to sneeze at. The toys and books are flying out of here. I've had to reorder for the candy aisle. Your decorating has been a huge success. People actually take family photos in front of your windows. They're that beautiful!" I said.

It was 1978 and these girls were making about $1.50 an hour in their paychecks.

I handed them each an envelope with a fifty dollar bill inside. They each got a copy of the company newsletter. Their photos and the letter I had written were on the front page of the red and white missive.

"You won!"

****

My Parent's Hands

"You've got two hands. Use them." my mother would say when I asked for something I could reach myself.

She'd also say that when I was a kid and didn't have any money to buy someone a present. I must have been pretty young because I had my own spending money since the age of twelve. That's when I got a paper route.

"You've got two hands. Use them. Get out your paper and markers. Make your own card. Make Auntie a pot holder on your loom. Paint a picture." she would encourage.

I'm not crafty. I never learned to knit or crochet. She hadn't either. I'm sure she would have taught me if she had. But, she was always willing to sit down and make a mess with me. Cutting up magazines. Turning socks into Barbie gowns.

I got married young. My husband and I found a huge apartment and rented it. We had dozens of windows with no curtains in them. We had large echoing rooms with a few sticks of furniture.

My mother took a look at all those empty windows and came for a visit. She plopped her sewing machine down on my vintage 50's kitchen table. The one she had found for me.

"Here. You'd better learn to use that, Little Girl. You'll go broke buying curtains and shades. If I remember right you can sew a straight seam. That's all curtains are after all.

Measuring and sewing straight seams. You have two hands. Use them." she said.

I taught myself how to make curtains.

My parents were invited to our new place for Christmas Eve dinner. Mom brought half the food. My father made trip after trip up the stairs carrying bags and boxes. I peered into cartons and found many things I didn't think I needed.

But, I ended up using everything eventually.

"I figured you didn't have a coffee pot. There's instructions inside on how to perk coffee. Go make your father some coffee while I put all this food away." she said.

Presents went under the tree. Trays of desserts went out onto the enclosed porch to stay cold. A big box remained in the middle of our living room waiting to be tripped over.

I ripped the tape off and found a handmade Christmas tree shaped wall hanging on top. My mother had made it out of cardboard egg cartons covered with shiny green garland. Little glass vintage balls were interspersed amongst the greenery. It hung flat on the wall. It plugged in and glowed.

It was so beautiful. Because she had made it for me.

"I figured you didn't have many Christmas decorations. Give me a few years and I'll give you all of mine. The older I get the less I put out. But, for now that looks pretty." my mother said as she saw her handmade tree fill the room with a soft light.

"Don't dig further into that box until your father is here." she said. "Ralph! Get in here. Darlene is going to open that box without you!"

My husband and father came around the corner from the kitchen. Each of them were sipping at cans of beer. My father had taken one mouthful of my first try at making coffee. He had spit it into the sink and cracked open the beer instead.

"Am I supposed to wait to open this, Daddy? It's not wrapped. Do I get to open it now?" I asked.

"Sure! I wanted to get you something for your first married Christmas. And your mother told me I had two hands. She told me to use them. So, I made you that." he said as I lifted a wooden manger out of the box.

The paper mache occupants of the crèche were familiar to me. They were the ones I hadn't been allowed to touch as a little girl.

My husband placed it on top of the shelving unit that held our television set. He plugged in the star light that lit the wooden barn like structure. I placed the figures in their places.

"Oh, and you'll need this too." Daddy said as he whipped a small baggie filled with straw out of his back pocket.

That was Christmas Eve 1978.

The tinsel tree ornament eventually succumbed to the years and the dampness of basement storage. But, I can close my eyes and visualize how beautiful it was the first time it adorned that bare apartment wall.

The wooden manger still exists and is used every Christmas. A framed photo of my parents sits alongside it every year now.

I miss them both very much.

My parents had loving hearts and hands. And, they used them.

****

Glimpses

Sometimes moments happen that let you glimpse into another person's soul. You can at least catch a glimpse of the little child they used to be. They are remarkable moments. They should be remembered.

My grandmother was an old Swedish lady. She never got too close to me. I don't know why. She was quiet. I was her son's daughter. I saw enough of her but I feel I never really ever knew her. She hardly ever tried to talk to me. Perhaps she was shy. I don't know.

She had a plastic bird on her kitchen window sill. When the container was filled with water the bird would bob all day long and drink out of a cylinder of water. It was a little bit of perpetual motion on a window sill. I never visited when I didn't see that plastic bird bobbing. It represented a hummingbird in shape. I never knew if she just got it going when I was coming for a visit or if she did it for herself. I'd like to think she did it for herself.

One Sunday I helped clear the table. I put dirty coffee cups into the sink. I stood to watch the bird bob away for a minute. I looked out the window at the real hummingbird feeder. Three beautiful turquoise hummingbirds hovered around it. They drank the sugar water and switched places.

I waved my arm behind me at my grandmother. She noticed the movement and came towards me. I slowed her down with my hand. I also used my hand to inch her forward towards the window. We watched the real birds together for a few moments. I glanced at her face and I saw the little girl she used to be so many years ago. She was enthralled. She didn't hide herself from me. I remember.

I never glimpsed into my grandfather in person. I only recognize him in the intricate little log cabins he built for my mother's Christmas village. I see him in the small flower shaped braided rugs he made. I still have one in my living room. He had big hands but he was an artist. I see him there in the things he made.

I recognized the boy that was my father every time we crested the hill that revealed Lake Champlain before us. He would drive right by the camp and park at the beach if he wasn't pulling a boat. He would get out of the car and drink it in. He didn't notice or care if we followed him out of the car. He was all alone with a group of people around him.

I glimpsed my mother as a girl whenever she was in the company of her oldest sister. She sat up straight. She minded her manners. She wanted to impress. She was a bit bossy with her youngest sister. But with Rita? She was all ears. She was willing to still learn with her.

My mother's childhood stories were full of The Depression. How could they not be? It was a very large family and times were very hard. We don't remember the easy times in sharp focus. We remember the hard times. These times were always overlaid with a lot of love. I never felt sorry for her when I heard them. Until I heard how hard she wished for a china doll one Christmas.

Ellie and her little brothers lay behind the wood cook stove. They wrote out a Christmas list on the back of an old roll of wallpaper. It must have been a pretty extensive list or they wrote really big.

Her mother took one look at this list and gathered them around her. She explained that Santa wasn't bringing non-essentials that year. There might be a new hat for someone that needed one. There might be new socks for the brother that had outgrown his. There might be some fruit and nuts. Santa wasn't doing dolls during The Depression.

Well, little Ellie had great belief in Santa. Money woes hadn't reached as far north as the North Pole. Santa was a saint. Santa was magic. She never forgot the disappointment of receiving mittens instead of a doll.

She even described the doll of her dreams. She should have arrived with a beautiful china face with red lips. She should have been wearing a black velvet dress with a lace collar. She also imagined a beautiful hat trimmed with fabric flowers. Instead she got mittens. I remembered.

I was living in Idaho and I was perusing a gift shop. I was away from Connecticut for two years. I would be back.

Hopefully, my mother actually believed me when I told her that. She looked like she had her doubts.

I needed to buy Christmas gifts early. They had to be wrapped and shipped across the country.

I came around a corner and there was a lovely china doll. It stood all by itself in a glass case. She was on a motorized pedestal that turned her around slowly. She was well lit. I stared at her. She jogged my memory. Oh! There is little Ellie's doll spinning around right in front of me.

She had a beautiful little girl face. Her lips were bright red. She wore black velvet with a white lace collar. She wore a small white hat that enveloped her face with fabric flowers. She was complete with perfect little white tights and patent leather shoes. She cost a mint.

I decided that I didn't want anything for Christmas that year. I didn't need anything except to buy that doll for my mother. The salesgirl found the box for me. I rehearsed my explanation for my husband in the car. "I know! It was crazy expensive! But, Santa doesn't need to bring me a thing this year. Except maybe a book. And some chocolate. Oh, and some earrings." You get the picture.

I was taking a writing class at the time. I eeked out time from my life as a mother of two small children to write a few times a week. Everyone in the house left me alone when they saw me sitting at the typewriter. "Mommy is doing her homework." It almost seemed to impress my little children. They tiptoed around me and watched Thunder Cats yet again. They even lowered the volume upon request.

I wrote a short story to accompany the doll on her journey to Connecticut.

I wrote a story set on Cambridge Street in Worcester, Massachusetts. Little Ellie was laying on her stomach behind the stove. She helped her little brothers write their lists to Santa. All the time knowing that Santa probably couldn't come through in such a fashion. I included her hopes and her dreams and her disappointment. I'm sure back then I finished the story in swooping sentimental fashion. My stories back in the day either made you weep or roll your eyes big time.

I'm sure my father got a flannel shirt and some wool socks.

I wrapped it all to go and mailed it off to Connecticut.

I got a thank you note from my mother. My mother was a little stilted when she used the written word. I felt that she had appreciated the doll but perhaps I had missed the mark. I hadn't written well enough in the story to find the little disappointed girl on Christmas morning all those years ago.

We visited Columbus Street when we finally gave up Idaho for upstate New York. I noticed the doll dressed in velvet on her stand in the spare bedroom upstairs. She was dusted but she didn't look loved. Oh, me and my big ideas I thought. I aimed but I surely missed with this one.

I came downstairs and found my father drinking coffee in the kitchen. My mother had gone out back to throw some bread for the birds. I could see that she was caught at the fence line chatting with a neighbor.

I sighed.

"What's your problem?" my father asked.

I told him I thought that doll would have meant more to Mom. I had poured her heart and my own into that story that accompanied the doll. Perhaps, I wasn't the writer I thought I was yet. I had a ways to go. I don't have time to work on it right now I told him.

"What are you talking about?" he asked in astonishment. "I thought your mother wrote to you?"

"She did. She said thank you very much. It was quite a surprise to receive a doll for Christmas. Thank you so much for thinking of me. Something along those lines." I said quietly as I made myself some tea.

"Your mother opened that box. She zeroed in on that doll. Her eyes got round. She said "Oh, my God." about

ten times in a row. She picked it up and she showed me.
She grabbed the doll and ran into the bedroom. She
slammed the door and cried for about ten minutes." he
said.

"Then she came out and read the story. She read it
outloud to me. I had to finish it for her. She was too
choked up. Then she took her doll and disappeared again.
I had to make my own breakfast." he said with a
harumph.

"She cried?" I wailed.

"Oh! It was a good cry. She came out with that doll and
put it next to the Christmas tree. She didn't stop grinning
all day long. That doll is usually on her bureau. But, she's
got three little granddaughters coming today. So, she put
it upstairs. She doesn't want three little girls fighting over
it. She doesn't want to say "That is my doll. Put it down.
You're not allowed to touch my doll. You have plenty of
dolls of your own. That's my only one and I waited a long
time for that doll." he finished.

We looked at each other and burst out laughing.

No wonder that black velvet dress didn't have any dust on
it.

****

Christmas Without My Mother

The words Mother and Christmas go together naturally. As they should. After my mother was gone? Christmas was never the same.

My mother died in mid November,1998. I was exhausted afterwards. I had been doing a show and I had to continue on in a musical comedy a day after my mother had passed from this life. I had to sing and dance and tell jokes for an audience. It was torturous.

I went on because I had promised to be on that stage and I was the lead. It was hard. It was impossible. But, I persevered. I heard her voice in my head saying that I had to go on. She was watching. She egged me on when exhaustion washed over me. Grief had me almost paralyzed and I had to dance. No makeup in the world could cover the black circles under my eyes.

The show was over at the end of November. Life went on as usual. Except nothing was usual anymore. Life couldn't be usual. My mother wasn't in it anymore. This life would never ever be the same because she wasn't in it.

Still I felt her close by. She would never leave me alone. Time after time she promised me that as a little girl. Those words weren't spoken when I was an adult but I remembered them.

I felt her around me. I dreamed of her. I noticed her when a cardinal would swoop by. I found her in a song on the radio. She even physically shoved me from behind in my kitchen a few times. I recognized the signs but I couldn't lift my chin above the bereavement.

I usually have an overabundance of Christmas spirit and decorations.

My children saw Christmas approaching and still I didn't dig out the lights for the front of the house. The Christmas tree could stay in it's box for all I cared. The myriad boxes of ornaments and Christmas villages stayed in the basement. There would always be next year. As far as I was concerned this would be a year without Christmas. I didn't have it in me.

My daughter looked me in the face over dinner one night. "Are you going to lose your Christmas spirit because Grammy is gone? That is not right!" she said. "She wouldn't like that at all! Where are your Christmas decorations? Why are there no lights on this house? Where is the village?"

I just looked at her and ate more salad. Not because I was hungry. I hadn't been hungry in a month. I ate because I knew I had to.

Winter was coming very slowly that year. We live on the outskirts of the Adirondack mountains. We usually have a white Christmas up to our knees at least. But, here it was the second week of December and still no snow.

I looked out at the bare yard and realized I'd never really taken care of the leaves that year. What with the show and my mother dying. I have neighbors that are particular about their yards. I should do something about the lawn for their sake while the snow held off and the weather pretended it wasn't winter.

I walked around with my mower with the bagger on. I sucked up leaves like a vacuum. I dumped and dumped the bag into the woods. It felt good to move. It felt good to stop crying. But, Christmas? Not this year. They'd have to figure out how to do that without me.

I took a rake and went after the side yard with the last of my energy. Another half an hour and then I would call it quits. I moved empty planters from the side of the house and got rid of the wet leaves. I went around the propane tanks. I turned to hit the opposite side of the area and that's when I saw them.

I was afraid to hurt them with the sharp ends of the rake. I knelt down and raked with my gloved hands. Soon I was using both hands. I uncovered yard upon yard of violets. My mother called them Johnny Jump Ups. They surrounded me.

She had brought me Johnny Jump Ups in plastic containers from a nursery the year we bought this house. I went to put them into a planter and she said no! You plant them in the yard and they will spread. They will be the first thing to nod their heads at you in the spring time. Just imagine! When you're sick of snow you will look and see their vibrant purple and yellow heads. You'll think of me.

I had planted them on the other side of our big yard. And now here they were. On the opposite side of the acre. In December. December! Beneath my fingers. I lay on my side on the ground and I cried until I was totally empty. I screamed at the trees. How could you leave me? It wasn't time for you to go!

I lay there for quite a while. There were no more tears. My body wouldn't give me any more even though I wanted them. I took my gloves off and I ran my palms over the velvet of the flowers. Over and over until it tickled. Until I laughed. Violets in December!

I got up and put away the rake. I went into the house and called my father. I told him about the dreams. I told him about the cardinals. I told him about the shoves at my back in the kitchen. Then, I told him about the violets. The violets in December. I reminded him of the day she gave them to me. How she had said when you see the violets "You'll think of me."

I couldn't promise him the flowers would still be there when he arrived. I arranged a day to pick him up and bring him to my house for Christmas. I promised him lots of lights. I promised him the Christmas village that my mother had given me. I hung up the phone.

I went into the garage and found the box of Christmas lights and started stringing them across the bushes.

****

Small Miracles Noticed

It was my birthday. It was mid November. The phone rang and my Daddy sang Happy Birthday at me. It was the first time that he had sung it alone. My mother had died the year before.

"I know this will be a hard birthday for you, Little Girl. Just remember. Sometimes the only thing you can change is your attitude." my Daddy said to me down the phone line.

It was perhaps the millionth time he'd told me his catch phrase about having a good attitude.

I hung up the phone. I hung my head. I had a cry. I made coffee. I was on the second cup as I gazed out my kitchen window. I talked with my mother in my head. She'd been hearing a lot from me. I was done yelling at her for dying and leaving us all.

"I know you believed in signs, Mom. I know your favorite was a bright red cardinal. How come I'm not seeing any cardinals in the back yard today, huh? It's my birthday. And, not one cardinal?" I thought.

So much for a good attitude.

I went to the mall to buy a skirt. I had an hour. That's where I met Irene.

She was a little old lady and she was lost in the mall. I accompanied her through the hallways. She seemed delicate. A little confused by the layout. I was mostly there as her way out of the maze. She had told me when I held the door open for her "I'm never going to remember where I put the car."

Forty five minutes in.............I finally asked her what exactly she was looking for.

She was looking for a cardinal.

I perked up. I led her to the store that sells Christmas ornaments in November. I told her about my mother and how I had hoped to see a cardinal that day. She grabbed me in a bear hug and she swayed back and forth with me. She held on a long time. I let her.

She leaned back and looked me in the face. "Oh, what a wonderful mother you must have had. How lucky were you? Your mother gave you beauty. Your mother gave you grace. Your mother gave you kindness. Oh, my goodness! You are blessed." Irene said.

The lady selling the cardinal ornaments handed Irene her ornament in a little paper bag with the temporary store's name on it.

She also handed me a small package with a bow on it.

"I'm such an eavesdropper. Forgive me. But, this is for you. On your birthday. From your mother." she said as she walked off to take care of two more customers.

Irene and I sat on a bench. Men were constructing Santa's Workshop in the middle of the mall. Power saws buzzed. Hammers whacked. I opened up the tissue paper. Nestled inside was a beautiful red cardinal ornament.

Irene held my hand while I cried.

Irene called me after that...............every year on my birthday. She sent me Christmas cards with cardinals on them. She came to see me in every show I was in. She got older and perhaps more lonely. The phone calls came more often.

"Did I ever tell you?" she said during her last phone call that came right before Christmas a few years ago. "No, I don't think I ever did."

"My husband died many years ago. He loved Christmas so much. I took care of him at home during the last year of his life. Sometimes he got so confused. The doctor said it was a touch of dementia." she explained.

"I was busy making Christmas Eve dinner. I heard him in the hallway closet. He had his coat on and he was searching for his boots. I said where do you think you're going? Dinner is almost ready." she remembered.

"That dear sweet man.....he said he had to get to the pet store............he wanted to buy me and my daughter kittens for Christmas. Oh, that dear, dear man." she said with a sniff.

"Well, I put a stop to that. He couldn't drive by himself anymore. And, dinner was coming out of the oven. And, that's all I needed. A brand new kitten with everything else that was going on in my life. So, I put him back in his recliner and told him that it was a wonderful thought. But, I didn't really want a kitten that year." she said.

"He forgot about it in a few minutes, thank God!" she ended.

"Oh, that was so sweet. Irene." I said. I thought she was done with her story.

"Oh, I'm not done yet." she continued. "He died that winter. It was a release, really. Oh, I missed him awful but it was a release. The next Christmas morning I was in the kitchen. I thought I heard a baby crying. It was the weirdest noise. I walked all around the downstairs with my ears perked up. I finally opened the front door...............and there was a little kitten sitting on the Welcome mat."

"I scooped it up. It was hungry and shaking with cold. That poor little kitten. But, I knew! I knew my husband was telling me not to be sad. And, he sent that kitten to me." she said.

"Oh, my God! That is fantastic! I've got goose bumps! No! You never told me this story before." I exclaimed.

"Oh, I'm not done yet." she said with the giggle of a young girl.

"So. I'm clutching this little kitten in one hand. I go to grab the phone with the other hand. I needed to call my daughter. To tell her that Daddy sent me a kitten for Christmas. When, the phone rang and I almost jumped out of my skin." she continued.

I picked the phone up. And, it was my daughter. She was so excited. She was talking a mile a minute. It seems she had just walked around her house trying to figure out what a strange noise was." Irene told me with excitement in her voice.

"Her father had sent her a kitten too."

****

This Christmas

Christmas is a time for family.

I'm ecstatic that my little family unit of four will be together for a week this holiday. I've promised myself that I will tell stories when the second glass of chardonnay hits my system. I'll take lots of photos. Of course, I won't be allowed to tag anyone in the photos on Facebook. We'll be in our pajamas for days. There won't be any makeup. We'll have bedhead. It's not going to be pretty.

Sounds like good times right?

A friend of mine was bemoaning her Christmas plans to me. It seems she enjoys her family. She just didn't like the early time they are all getting together. She was bereft that she was going to have to forego her yoga pants. "I'll have to actually put on pants that have a waist band. We eat like little piggies and I'll have a metal button poking into my belly. I am not looking forward to that." she said.

"Give everyone a call. Turn it into a pajama party Christmas. Only sleep pants allowed. Slippers. Tee shirts decorated with Garfield and Snoopy. It will be a new tradition. You'll be a hero." I suggested.

She looked interested but I don't think she has the nerve. That's really too bad. She would have become part of family folk lore. "In 2016 your Great Great Aunt had a terrific idea. Here is the plaque with her name on it." children of future generations would be told.

And there she would be on that bronze plaque. Frozen forever with her hair in a messy ponytail on the top of her head. Fuzzy slippers and drawstring p.j. bottoms emblazoned with characters from the Flintstones.

A hero.

I was born in 1957. I was a little girl during the sixties. I have a pretty terrific memory. I didn't keep a diary. My brain is full of snapshots I'll never forget. I drank up conversations and stories. I paid attention.

I spent stilted but loving Christmas Eve's at my grandparents house in Glastonbury. They were Swedish. Their Christmas traditions were lovely but not as involved as I was used to. I drank coffee with them at an early age. I ate cookies made with a press dipped in hot oil. They were shaped like flowers and stars and filled with raspberry jam. Sprinkled with powdered sugar.

There was no talk of Santa Claus. I think my Swedes were a little too serious minded for such silliness. There was quiet. There were candles lit on the dining room table with it's linen table cloth. There were Canadian mints in a glass candy dish.

My grandmother would touch the dish and take off the top. She'd wink at me when my mother wasn't looking. She'd rustle the candy with the tip of her finger and turn her back. It was a strange invitation. But, I took it to mean "Have some candy. Your mother probably won't like you full of sugar at this time of night. I'm not going to ask permission. She's my daughter-in-law and I don't mess with her rules. But………..it is my house………..and I did buy these for you……………."

I always had a hard time sleeping on Christmas Eve. It wasn't just the excitement. I was buzzing with sugar. And, coffee.

Christmas Day brought us to church early in the morning. And, then my mother's relatives would arrive. She had so many brothers and sisters I don't think she even knew exactly how many she had. They were fun. They were loud. They always made two trips from the car carrying food and presents.

We lived in a tiny house on Columbus Street. That house was bursting with people. Spare tables were set up. You couldn't eat in the kitchen because every surface was covered in food.

Cousins slid around in their stocking feet over head. The wooden floors were new and glossy. Perfect for sock skating. They bashed into walls quite often. The group of mothers would stop and listen. If they didn't hear glass breaking..............they'd just keep talking.

The basement was full of men drinking beer kept cold in the hatchway. They played pool and got boisterous.

Men ate too much and leaned back and unbuttoned their pants. Ahhh! Belch. The women knew they had put on a good spread.

The women arrived in tight black skirts. Christmas sweaters and brooches. High heels that my mother wouldn't let past the throw rug in the kitchen. They made punch marks on her highly glossed linoleum floor. She'd hand all the ladies woolen slippers made by my Swedish grandmother. Their patent leather show off shoes were lined up underneath the kitchen radiator.

After eating it was time for the women to band together to do the dishes and put away the leftovers. All men disappeared during this hour. Poof! Gone. Most children did the same thing. They'd rather play basketball on a driveway covered in snow than get roped into drying the dishes.

I stuck with the aunties. No one could move for awhile from over feeding and too tight undergarments. One auntie would start it. She'd stick her hands down her sleeves and wrestle a little with her brassiere. Off it would come through the arm hole of her sparkling sweater. She'd wave it over her head.

"Free! Free at last!" she'd declare to the crowd of females. They'd cheer and run for my mother's bedroom. There they would divest themselves of bras. And girdles. Yes, girdles. Whalebone was a thing of the past but girdles still existed. They'd come out wearing my mother's softest oldest hang around the house clothing.

Then they'd do the dishes.

They'd laugh. And catch up. And gossip. And tell stories.

I was there to put things away where they belonged. And, listen.

One of their favorite stories was about the Indian Princess in the family. "Was it Ma's mother? Or, grandmother?" one sister would ask. They'd argue about that for a few minutes. I'm thinking it was their great grandmother. You don't lose track of a grandmother that quickly. Not with that many females remembering.

She was of the Nipmuc tribe. Except they could never remember the word Nipmuc. It could have been Micmac. But, they had heated discussion and came up with Nitwit. Which was closer to Nipmuc. They'd call an uncle not in attendance and ask him.

He'd yell "NIPMUC!" over the phone line. "Why can't you remember this? Will you write it down?" he demanded before he banged the phone down.

Then the photo of their mother would come down off of my parent's bedroom wall. They'd look her square in the eye. They'd get weepy missing her. They told me stories about her. I stared at that photo as they remembered her.

"She would have loved you." the aunties would tell me.

I'd get misty eyed myself while looking at the photo of the lady I'd never met. Would never meet. I'd trace her high sharp cheek bones with my forefinger. I saw the Native American in her.

I remember all those Christmases. The aunties and uncles that put on their best clothes and brought their culinary treats. The cousins that I loved to play with. I could never get enough of all of them.

I appreciate their efforts to be together on holidays even if they had to travel. I loved the noise. I remember who fell asleep during home movie hour. I remember who told the best stories. The gossip that I wasn't supposed to hear. I remember being loved.

Most of those dear people are gone now. I miss them.

My brother wrote to me yesterday. He shared the results of a DNA test he had done. I wasn't surprised at being 52 percent Scandinavian. I thought the 26% Irish was a little low. I was surprised at the 6% Russian. The 1% Asian was an eye opener.

I was devastated that there was no Native American in him. My full blooded brother. Not a trace of Nipmuc is in his blood according to this saliva test.

The storyteller in me questions these results.

I was born a storyteller. I come from a long line of them. I listened to stories in that little kitchen on Columbus Street. My aunties weren't making up their Nipmuc ancestor. She was too real to them. I saw her for myself in the face of my own grandmother.

The DNA test doesn't matter. It's not important. I can't be convinced that this woman wasn't real. That she didn't belong to all of us.

She will remain in my stories. I will tell them. I will most certainly write them.

I ask that you do the same for your family. This Christmas.

Put on your favorite sweatpants in front of company. Get comfy. Eat too much. Drink one too many. Laugh loudly. Cry a little while missing someone that is no longer with you. Get out your camera. Take lots of photos. Especially of your relative that tries to hide from the lens. Write down your favorite family story.

Today becomes tomorrow very quickly. You are making memories right now.

Be the storyteller.

I wish I knew how to say that in Nipmuc.

****

Santa Squirrel Takes Care Of Business

Christmas magic. Oh, there was a time..............when the kids would get excited. They'd beg me to put up the Christmas tree. I told them that perhaps...........we'd do Halloween and Thanksgiving first.

I understood their excitement. I know Santa for the saint he is. I passed on my love for him and all things nativity after all.

But, still they had to wait.

I wasn't above using good Old St. Nick for my own benefit. Oh, I didn't creep the kiddies out with the whole "He sees you when you're sleeping, he knows when you're awake" thing. I didn't like that when I was a kid.

I know for a fact that Santa is not a stalker.

But, when a kid wanted an expensive toy in the mall? And, it was mid November? I kept my check book safely tucked into the zip up compartment of my purse.

I'd snort and say, "No way! Did you take out the trash last night? Nope. Did you clean all the dirty underwear and socks out from under your bed? Nope. If you want that toy I guess you'd better ask Santa. And, you'd better straighten up your act. Because, I know how to write letters to Santa too. I'm not saying I'd rat you out…………but…………."

Things change. Kids grow up. But, I don't. I don't change much. Ask my hair dresser.

I will never grow up if that means I can't have a six foot Easter Tree in my living room.

But, my children became adults. They like Christmas alright. But not to the extent of ……………owning a snowman collection. A cardinal collection. Three different Christmas villages. Cookie exchange parties. Christmas girl sleepovers. Walking through hip deep snow to put up blinking lights.

A wreath on the door will do it for them.

Gone are the days when their wish lists grew longer by the hour. Lists so long I had to have them highlight MUST HAVE in yellow, REALLY WANT in pink and WILL DIE IF I DON'T GET in orange.

Now, I sit at home begging……………yes I have resorted to actually begging……………for a Christmas wish list from these two.

It starts with an email. "Hey, I know it's early……………but you live far away………………and that good old post office has been known to take their good old time……………so………could you please send me a list of what you'd like for Christmas? Or, do you just want money? I could do that if you'd like. Or, half and half. Just let me know in the next day or two."

Radio……….phone……….computer silence.

Talking in the wind.

The second email asks if they got the first email.

A quick response comes. "Yes, got it. Still thinking about it. Geesh, Mom. Christmas is what? Six weeks away? Chill! Love you and have some patience, Your Child."

I let another week pass.

This time I go for the personal touch. A phone call. We catch up on what's new. What show are you doing? How is the cat? That sort of thing. But, I eventually get to what I really want to know.

I ask for a Christmas list. I stand by with a pad of paper and a pen in my hand. Again, I am disappointed.

All I get is a list of reasons why this child of mine doesn't know what they want for Christmas yet.

I wait another few days.

And, then? I get inventive.

I poke around in a closet. I come up with a stuffed animal. Okay, it's a squirrel. I have an affinity for squirrels. I like to feed them chocolate macaroons and watch them scale tall buildings. Leap over sheds. Pass out under the pine trees.

For some God forsaken reason my husband gave me a stuffed squirrel last Christmas.

Probably, because he begged for a Christmas list and I didn't give him one.

I pull out the red wooden sleigh that my grandfather built for me when I was a little girl. I fill it with shiny glass ornaments. I plop the squirrel's buttocks among the balls. I balance him so he sits up straight and tall.

I take a photograph.

I take a good hour to figure out how to attach one stinking photo to an email. (I know..........but it happens every time.) I write a little message designed to irk my overly busy grown up children.

The email says:

Hello, My name is Santa Squirrel.
Your mother has hired me to do her dirty business. She is up to her eyeballs in work and writing and baking and Christmas parties she doesn't really want to go to. She's running out of time for shopping. Especially online shopping for people that are 6'5"inches tall. All the other extraordinarily tall people are already buying up all the clothing at the Big and Tall stores.

I have also been told to notify you that packages are mailed by either US Postal Service or UPS. The post office and UPS people are liars. Oh, they say they'll get it there in two days. But, they don't mean it. They actually wink when they say it. The whole reindeer delivering to you on Christmas Eve? Well, you need to snap out of it and grow up. Santa is real but reindeer? Well, just grow up.

If a detailed list is not received by noon tomorrow you will be getting only one gift this year.

And, you are looking at a photo of it. You will be getting a slightly lopsided stuffed squirrel and a bag full of scratched up cheap plastic ornaments.

You will not be getting the wooden sleigh that I am sitting in. Not until your mother is gone. She may leave it to you in her will. Oh, hell, what she really said was "Over my dead body."

With Some Love and Much Impatience, Santa Squirrel

I finally figured out how to attach that photo and the email was on it's way.

I received detailed wish lists within hours.

My daughter attached a note for Santa Squirrel.

"Dear Santa Squirrel, I love you. You are beautiful. Just looking at you makes me happy. Do you want to come and live at my house? I think you'd be very content here." she wrote.

Santa Squirrel wrote back to her immediately.

"Nuts to you." he wrote in rude squirrel fashion.

But, then he lightened up because the Christmas spirit was strong.

"Why don't you buy yourself a plane ticket and come for a visit? Come and meet me in person. Your mother has promised to make cookies that no one will eat. She always gives them to the back yard squirrels on New Years Eve. Love, S. Squirrel."

****

The Memories That Make Us

Memories. They are precious stuff. My good memories crowd out the bad. It might be about attitude. It might be that I try to find some good even in the bad. I don't know.

I'm not really that wise.

I have gotten to a certain age though. I'm old enough to know a day full of memories when it's happening. I pay attention. I drink it in. I might even be surprised that those around me don't realize the importance of the moment they're in. That's okay. It's all part of the experience.

Christmas takes planning. Wonderful holiday memories don't usually just happen on their own. Sometimes they do though. Those are precious holiday treats.

Like the time…………I dragged my whole family to midnight mass on Christmas Eve. The kids were crabby and squirming. The priest starting swinging the incense. My little boy said out loud that something "Smells fishy to me!" Really loudly. My husband is an early morning person. He was almost slapping himself to stay awake through the mass that took us from Christmas Eve into Christmas Day.

I didn't sing with the church choir that year. I usually did. The choir had been removed from the choir loft and placed on the altar with the priest and the sacraments. I didn't go for that.

It's hard to explain. Maybe I'm an old fashioned girl. Maybe I think the congregation should have to sneak peeks behind their backs to see who is singing in the loft that day. I'm thinking I mostly didn't like being put on display as if I was performing in a show.

I do enough of that. Buy a ticket.

We sat in a pew in the middle of the church. We sang along to all the songs interspersed throughout the hour. I've always enjoyed singing church music. Most of it has been written in my key. I shut my eyes and sway and let it rip.

I have a pretty voice. It's somewhat trained. I doubt very much that you're going to run out and by my CD however.

We got to the part in the mass where we all shake hands and wish each other peace. The woman in front of me turned around at that point with tears streaming down her face. She knelt on her pew. She grabbed me and hugged me and swayed back and forth with the pew pressing into my stomach.

Okay. We're making memories here. I had no idea who she was but she obviously needed a big weeping hug right at that very moment.

The "I wish you Peace" and the "Merry Christmas" wishing took longer than usual during that mass. Father was out in the crowd pressing hands and slapping backs. So the woman had time to tell me what this was all about.

She was about sixty and very pretty in her Christmas sweater and pin.

"This is my first Christmas midnight mass without my mother. She died this year. I miss her so much. She lived with me for the last ten years of her life. Today.........I was so depressed. I sat in my kitchen and thought I can't do it. I can't go to midnight mass without my mother. And, then her voice was in my head. And, she said "I have a gift for you. You have to go to mass tonight. Look for your gift. It will be right behind you." she explained to me.

She talked very fast.

"And?" I asked. I looked around. I guess I expected to see a foil wrapped gift with a big bow on a pew somewhere nearby.

"You! You are my gift! My mother had a beautiful pure soprano voice. Just like yours. I sat here and I closed my eyes. I could swear my mother was right behind me. You are my gift." she said as she wiped her face with her hands.

I've never been so flattered and touched and creeped out at the same time. There's a memory for you.

Like the time..................I was singing at Christmas mass. Up in the choir loft. The choir loft that made me wonder how much weight it could really hold. (Perhaps a building inspector answered that question and that's why the choir ended up on the altar. Hmmm.....just thought of that.)

I was wearing a Christmas pin made by Avon that my mother had given me. It was about two inches wide. Three white candles surrounded by greenery and red berries. You pressed a little button and the candles blinked in turn. I had activated it in the car to entertain my son. I had forgotten to turn it off.

We got to the point in the mass where Father gets up and gives the sermon that he's worked on all week. He was trying to do it without notes. With feeling. Except he turned around at that point with tears streaming down her face. She knelt on her pew. She grabbed me and hugged me and swayed back and forth with the pew pressing into my stomach.

Okay. We're making memories here. I had no idea who she was but she obviously needed a big weeping hug right at that very moment.

The "I wish you Peace" and the "Merry Christmas" wishing took longer than usual during that mass. Father was out in the crowd pressing hands and slapping backs. So the woman had time to tell me what this was all about.

She was about sixty and very pretty in her Christmas sweater and pin.

"This is my first Christmas midnight mass without my mother. She died this year. I miss her so much. She lived with me for the last ten years of her life. Today………I was so depressed. I sat in my kitchen and thought I can't do it. I can't go to midnight mass without my mother. And, then her voice was in my head. And, she said "I have a gift for you. You have to go to mass tonight. Look for your gift. It will be right behind you." she explained to me.

She talked very fast.

"And?" I asked. I looked around. I guess I expected to see a foil wrapped gift with a big bow on a pew somewhere nearby.

"You! You are my gift! My mother had a beautiful pure soprano voice. Just like yours. I sat here and I closed my eyes. I could swear my mother was right behind me. You are my gift." she said as she wiped her face with her hands.

I've never been so flattered and touched and creeped out at the same time. There's a memory for you.

Like the time………………I was singing at Christmas mass. Up in the choir loft. The choir loft that made me wonder how much weight it could really hold. (Perhaps a building inspector answered that question and that's why the choir ended up on the altar. Hmmm…..just thought of that.)

I was wearing a Christmas pin made by Avon that my mother had given me. It was about two inches wide. Three white candles surrounded by greenery and red berries. You pressed a little button and the candles blinked in turn. I had activated it in the car to entertain my son. I had forgotten to turn it off.

We got to the point in the mass where Father gets up and gives the sermon that he's worked on all week. He was trying to do it without notes. With feeling. Except he kept staring at the choir loft. His voice would run out. He'd strain his neck and stare up at the choir. He'd shake his head and try to pick up where he left off. It happened over and over again.

He was usually a very eloquent speaker. With a few bad jokes sprinkled throughout. I mean we'd all laugh. The guy was trying so hard and he was so sweet. But, that night he'd cock his head like a cocker spaniel. He'd stare at the choir and lose it. He'd stop talking all together.

I realized in time that he was trying to figure out what the blinking light was up there. I put my hand over the Avon Christmas pin as I searched for the off button. He regained his composure and gave his sermon the big finish he had planned.

Father came up the choir loft stairs after mass. He gave each member of the choir a bottle of St. Nicholas rose wine. The most terrible wine ever pressed but the bottle was pretty.

He glanced at my Christmas vest with the pin attached.

"Lose the pin next year and Merry Christmas." he said to me as he handed me a bottle of wine with a big grin on his face.

Like the time....................I scrubbed and I cleaned. I almost tied the kids up in a corner so they wouldn't mess up the rooms I had shined. I baked. I cooked. Then I put on my Christmas sweater and stood near the door waiting for my parent's car to arrive for their extended holiday visit. I stood there and smiled and greeted them as if my house was always this clean and perfect.

We were a day into our visit when the wind blew and screamed around the house. The power went out.

It didn't come back for two days.

We put wood into the wood stove. We melted buckets of snow for the toilets. We packed food into coolers and buried them in snow banks. We lit candles. We found fuel for the Coleman lanterns.

We told stories. We played games. We ate and piled up dirty dishes. We sang songs. We had a two day long card game.

My mother lived to play cards. Her greeting upon arrival was always "Whose deal?". My father liked it almost as much as she did although he didn't win as often as my mother did.

The kids got their blankets. They got games and story books. They slept around our feet. They were happy just to be with us. They'd watched enough Little House On The Prairie to think of this as an adventure.

My mother sighed with happiness as she played cards with the lantern sitting in the middle of the table.

"I know this isn't exactly what you had planned, Darlene. But, I have to tell you…………these two days in the dark………….playing cards………….have been two of the happiest days of my life. I'll never forget it. What a memory." she said.

She meant it. And, we all agreed.

Like the time……………just last week. My daughter arrived for a nine day Christmas visit.

She lives so far away that it makes my soul hurt sometimes. Those are the moments I remember how much she loves where she is. How much she loves her husband and her kitty cat. What a good job she's found and I am happy for her.

Now, I'm glad that she is going out of her way to come to see us for nine days. Because she misses us. Because she loves us.

What does she want to do when she's here? Nothing. She wants to stay in. She wants to wear pajamas day and night. She wants Daddy to cook for her. She wants to play board games. Power watch Netflix. Maybe she'll build a snow man.

She just wants to be with us.

And, that's what we all did.

We stayed up late just talking. We slept in. We ate and drank wine. We played games and watched movies. Our daughter relaxed and was happy. She sang to the cat. She sang Christmas songs when she thought she was alone.

I usually have to travel to the west coast to hear her sing. I have to buy a ticket. It's what she does.

Every evening I was the last to go to bed. I laughed to myself while I remembered my daughter singing "Do You Want To Build A Snowman?" to my unfriendly cat. The cat had actually hissed in her face. I guess she really did not want to build a snow man.

Memories came to me. Memories of Christmas past. A woman who cried upon hearing me sing. A priest that gave me wine after I almost made him lose his mind during his sermon. My parents playing cards for days at Christmas and how they enjoyed it more than all our cancelled plans.

My mother saying that those two days doing not much of anything............were two of the happiest days of her life.

I just spent a week doing not much of anything. And, they are some of the happiest days of my life.

These memories make me who I am. May I continue to make them and cherish them. May I never lose them. I know! I will write them down

Perhaps............. I really am wise after all.

****

Flying With Mary Poppins

I've had many jobs in my life. The one I found to be my profession or my calling has been being a mother. I've always taken great joy in my two children. I didn't need to be told "Enjoy these days. They're the best days of your life when your children are small." I knew it when I was living it.

My son and daughter have given me many gifts during their life times. I've saved their handmade Mother's Day cards and the drawings that used to decorate the refrigerator. They graduated to thoughtful store bought gifts. They add to my cardinal collection. I also seem to be collecting Mickey Christmas ornaments. I don't know how that happened but I love them.

They fill my jewelry box with pretty trinkets. My son asked me what I wanted for Christmas this year as he was leaving for the mall. I waved him off with "Oh, I don't know. Surprise me with something shiny and glittery."

I opened an emerald necklace on Christmas morning. I opened my mouth to say "Oh! you shouldn't have spent so much on me!" but I shut it again because it was so beautiful. He got joy buying it for me. I am too terrified to wear it. I tend to lose jewelry. I do crack that little black velvet box open every morning just to touch it, though.

All the gifts have been thoughtful. It took me a few minutes to wrap my head around the thoughtfulness of my son's new tattoo though. He showed it to me and I screeched "Tell me that's not real. Tell me that is temporary!" He had gotten my name encircled by a red heart on his upper arm.

"Why would you do such a thing?" I yelled in his face.

"Why? Why? Because you are my favorite person in the world and I wanted your name on my arm. Get used to it Ma!" he answered.

That shut me up quick. Now, once in a while I'll blurt out "Show me my tattoo, Andy! I need a lift right now." He'll roll up his sleeve and flash that heart in my face and smile.

My son lives here. My daughter? All the way across the country in Oregon. She is an actress and we try to get out there once a year to catch her in a show. I've seen her portray many characters. Last year she landed the role of Mary Poppins.

It was a Christmas production running for about six weeks at a terrific theater that gears their season to children. I figure almost a thousand children a day were seeing her fly as Mary Poppins. We couldn't get away. They sold out without us. I was feeling left out.

I read the first review on line and it was a good one. My daughter was "born for this role." She and her Bert made the reviewer "forget all about Dick Van Dyke and Julie Andrews." Can't get much better than that.

I printed out the review so my husband could read it later. I wasn't satisfied. I imagined blinking my eyes, crossing my arms and transporting myself all the way to Oregon. Like I Dream of Jeanie. I wouldn't even take time to leave a note. My husband would come home and say "Now, where the heck is she off too? What? No dinner?"

I felt like a good whine. But, there was no one home to whine to. The cat pays no attention to me when I whine.

My parents are gone now. They were good parents so their voices and advice still linger. I don't want you thinking I hear voices in my head. I don't run around in my underwear chasing butterflies. But, I always listened to them. I remember.

At that moment I heard Dad say "Well, sometimes you can't change a situation. All you can really change right now is your attitude. It's all about attitude." Not cutting it right now, Dad. I'm feeling left out and pitiful. I want to be in Oregon. I want to see Mary Poppins fly.

Then my mother piped up with "Suck it up. Whining never got you anywhere. It's certainly not getting you anywhere right now." She was almost always right. She was aggravating that way.

I'd had a quick phone call from my daughter the night before. She was so busy it didn't last long. The show was going great. The audiences were loving it. They were selling out. She loved meeting and greeting the little kids after the show. The kids were sweet; the parents not so much. Shoving their kids to the front of the line. And her feet were absolutely killing her.

"I can't even feel my right foot by the end of the show, Mom! These Mary Poppins boots make the balls of my feet go numb. And, when they fly me that harness hurts. You would not believe the strange places I have bruises."

I remembered that conversation and got on the internet and ordered her special gel insoles. They're specially made for ladies wearing high heels. They cushion the ball of your foot. I hit overnight shipping and grimaced. But, it made me feel good to do something for her from so far away. I couldn't do anything about the harness except pray "Please, don't drop her on her head."

I got a cup of coffee and started poking around Google. I found another review. I tripped across a few publicity photos that I hadn't seen before. Then I came across a "Study Guide for Mary Poppins." It was something the theater came up with so the school children could turn a day at the theater into a lesson. Good way to get the School Board to pay for a bus load of kids to go see Mary Poppins fly. Teachers are smart that way.

It had a section on the Edwardian Age in London. It had a section on the author with a list of all the Mary Poppins books. It described the life of a chimney sweep. It described women's roles and what a nanny did for a family. It had an interview with my daughter.

Her answer to number 5 caught my attention and became one of the sweetest gifts I've ever received.

5. Do you know anyone like Mary Poppins? Or have you had a teacher, care taker or other who reminds you of Mary?

My mother is a little like Mary Poppins in that she always makes mundane things seem magical. She is one of the best storytellers I know. When I was younger she would tell bedtime stories so grand that you could believe that you had jumped into a chalk drawing or journeyed to the stars.

She and my father are very encouraging like Mary Poppins. They always told me and my brother that anything could happen. There were times in my youth when I wanted to be a scientist, others when I wanted to be an actor or even the President of the United States. They were always very clear that I could do any of those things if I wanted to. I only had to believe that it could happen and work towards those goals wholeheartedly.

I still look to my parents for encouragement and advise even though I'm grown. I think it's wonderful that our story shows a family growing together and communicating. By the end of the show, you know that the Banks children will be able to count on their parents even when they are older.

This gift from my daughter was unexpected. It didn't cost her anything. What made it most precious is that she probably never thought I'd see that in a million years. I wiped the tears from my eyes and glanced at the clock. I did the time difference math in my head. I figured she was flying across the stage holding her umbrella up over her head right about then.

I was flying too. Only, I didn't need an umbrella.

****

This is perhaps the most important Christmas story I've ever told. Without it..........well, I wouldn't be here to tell my stories.

When Ralph Met Ellie

My father visited for a week at a time at my house when he got old. My mother was gone and my brother and I met at a halfway point. I'd bring Daddy here for a holiday or for the week that my brother flew out on a vacation. Daddy would be here with me and my brother could relax in that knowledge.

I'm not the world's greatest cook. I reserve that title for my husband. But, I am the everyday keep em' alive cook. Everything is edible and tasty. I just don't get out recipe books. I have little imagination. My father loved my cooking; especially my meatloaf.

We never rushed to clear the table after dinner. That is when my father would remember when. He might tell a story over and over. I listened like it was the first time I'd heard it. He deserved that respect. But, once in a while a new story would drift across his memory. It was like hitting gold.

I didn't grab a pad of paper and keep notes. But, I'd tell myself to remember this. Pay attention and remember this.

My mother had told me a long time ago that she hung out with a group of young people in her youth. One of the young men liked her a lot. His name was Ronald.

"My God, he was crazy about me. I liked him a lot too. He was perhaps the nicest man I have ever met. But, I just couldn't get over the fact that he was also the homeliest man I'd ever seen too. I feel awful saying that. It makes me feel so shallow. But, I guess I have to say it. It's the truth. I had no interest in the nicest man God ever created because I couldn't imagine looking at his poor face every day." she confessed.

"But, he eventually gave up and was happy just being my friend. Another girl in the group was just crazy for him. She was sick of pretty boys that treated her like dirt. She thought Ronald was the most wonderful man. And, when you love someone like that? Well, let's just say she thought he was the most handsome man in the world. As it should be when two people love each other." she said. She smiled remembering the two of them together.

"I was a bridesmaid in their wedding." she added.

"So, Ronald says to me I've met a guy at work. He's from Maine but he lives and works in Worcester now. He's a

Swede named Ralph. I think you two would like each other a lot. I'll bring him bowling with me on Saturday. Will you be there? I don't want to get his hopes up that he's going to meet a nice girl if you won't be there." my mother explained.

"I got a little more information out of him about this Ralph the Swede. He sounded nice. He sounded like he missed his family. He sounded like he worked hard. So, I met him at the bowling alley and that's that." she ended.

I let my mother's voice take the beginning of this story because my father knew nothing about it. His story started the minute he laid eyes on her in a bowling alley.

"So, Ronald says he's got a nice young woman for me to meet. He's liked her for a long time but she's not interested. He's moved on. He has a pretty fiance. But, everyone still goes bowling together on a Saturday night. I walked into that bowling alley and Ronald pointed Ellie out to me. I almost turned and left the building." he said with a smile.

"What? Why Daddy? Why would you want to run from the building?" I asked with a laugh.

He got that certain soft smile on his face. Whenever he smiled that particular smile you knew he was thinking of his Ellie.

"Because. She was the most beautiful girl I'd ever seen. She looked like a movie star. How could a girl that beautiful possibly be interested in me? She was standing in the middle of all those young people. She was telling them a story. She was so bright she sparkled. They laughed at what she was saying. They all loved her. I turned to Ronald and said "Oh, I don't know. A girl like that will never be interested in me." He just laughed at me and said "Oh, I don't know Anderson. You're not so bad looking! Throw your shoulders back and put a smile on your face. Don't be afraid of her. She's that beautiful! But, she's beautiful on the inside too." he remembered outloud.

"I wonder if I ever thanked him." he said quietly as he took a sip of his alcohol free chardonnay. "I hope I thanked him. I can't imagine my life without Ellie. You wouldn't be sitting here, Little Girl if it wasn't for Ronald. I hope I thanked him."

"So, go on Daddy! Was it love at first sight? Did you love each other at first sight with all those people around in that noisy bowling alley?" I prompted him on.

He looked at me and laughed. "Oh, I loved her at first sight. I don't think she did. She was an awful lot like you, Little Girl. She wasn't impressed when some boy stuttered at her because she was so pretty. She was used to that. She used to say that you were a lot like her.

Neither one of you were boy crazy. You both decided after a little bit if someone wasn't for you. You two didn't waste a guy's time. That's why your mother and I believed you when you said you loved Young Mike here after only a few weeks. We never worried that you didn't mean it or that you were moving too fast. You met him? And bam. You were done looking." he said as he smiled at my husband.

"What's the first thing you said to her?" I asked in a dreamy fashion.

"Oh, I'm sure I was introduced around and she said it's nice to meet you or some such thing." he said as he tapped his wine glass for more. "I seem to remember sitting next to her on the bench and she asked me if I was always so quiet." He was trying very hard to remember.

"Oh! I know! She asked me about my family. If I missed them a lot. Your mother was very family oriented. I don't think she could imagine being so far away from her brothers and sisters. I remember taking out my wallet and I showed her the pictures I had of my sisters. I told her a little bit about each of my sisters." he said. He shook his head yes in the knowledge that he was remembering correctly.

"I told her I was planning a trip back to Maine in a few months. I was kind of stupid. I could have been rushing things a bit. I said I thought she'd love to see that part of Maine. Maybe, she'd like to come with me sometime. I remember she said something along the lines of maybe I'd take her out for a coffee or something before I tried to whisk her off to another state." he said with a chuckle.

Then came the part of the story that I loved so much. He told us how they had eventually broken off from the group to do things just the two of them.

"I would trot over and walk her home from work. There was a cafe diner sort of place. I told her I was hungry and I would buy her a sandwich or something. She would always say no. She had a big lunch that day. She would sit there talking away while I ate. She'd have a cup of tea or something. I thought she might be hungry. But, she would not let a man buy her anything. Her father had told her that if you let a man buy you something like a meal or a drink? They thought you owed them something. I didn't know that until later. She would just say no, I'm not hungry. But, I'll sit with you." he said as he smiled his Ellie smile.

"So, one night I dropped her off at her house. I think I was allowed in to say hello to her mother. Then I went across the street to wait for a bus. I was tired of walking. That's when I saw the light come on in their pantry. The curtain wasn't closed against the darkness yet. I watched while Ellie went into the pantry and started shoving crackers into her mouth. She was so hungry she didn't take food and sit down. She was standing there looking around and shoving food into her mouth. I went up to the window and tapped on the glass. She turned around and saw me. Her mouth was full of crackers and cheese. I said through the window pane "I thought you weren't hungry? " I'll never forget the look on her face! She was mortified that I had caught her. But, we laughed like hell about that later on. The next time I picked her up from work she let me buy her a meatloaf dinner." he laughed as he remembered.

"Now, I was being invited in on a Friday night. All her brothers and sisters were musical. They all played guitars together. Ellie would get on the piano. They'd sing and they'd laugh and I was part of it." he said with a happy sigh. "They treated me like part of the gang. Some of them were off on their own with husbands and wives. They'd all come and bring something to eat and share. I'd bring a big jar of pickles that they all loved so much. I might bring some beer. Those were happy days on Cambridge Street. And she let me be part of it."he added.

"So, Ronald asked me how it was going with Ellie one day at work. I said I was crazy about her. That my weekends with her family were great. That she would really only let me take her for walks. She didn't want to go anywhere that cost money. But, she had let me buy her a meatloaf dinner. I thought that was worth mentioning for some reason." he said.

"She let you buy her dinner? She let you pay for it?" roared Ronald. He clapped me on the back and said "You're doing great, Ralph. That girl never lets a guy buy her anything. She let you buy her meatloaf? Woo hooo!" he chuckled as he remembered that part.

"I don't know. She was skittish. She liked me a lot I could tell. But, I wasn't hurrying her. I didn't ask her to be my girlfriend or anything. I knew your mother wouldn't go for that. She didn't want anyone laying claim to her. I didn't have a lot of experience with girls but I could tell that. I just tried to make her happy." he explained.

"Meanwhile, her oldest brother Jimmy was speaking up for me. I didn't know it until a lot later. There were still a lot of young men swarming around Cambridge Street. She had just broken off writing to some soldier. Her brother Jimmy told her there were too many boys around. That people were going to start to talk. He told her it was time she picked one. He said I think you should go for the Swede. He is a hard worker. He loves his family. He loves you as much as I do. You can't do better than the Swede. I always liked that Jimmy." he said with a laugh.

"And then Christmas was coming. It got really cold out. We walked everywhere. She was never dressed warmly into her mouth. She was so hungry she didn't take food and sit down. She was standing there looking around and shoving food into her mouth. I went up to the window and tapped on the glass. She turned around and saw me. Her mouth was full of crackers and cheese. I said through the window pane "I thought you weren't hungry? " I'll never forget the look on her face! She was mortified that I had caught her. But, we laughed like hell about that later on. The next time I picked her up from work she let me buy her a meatloaf dinner." he laughed as he remembered.

"Now, I was being invited in on a Friday night. All her brothers and sisters were musical. They all played guitars together. Ellie would get on the piano. They'd sing and they'd laugh and I was part of it." he said with a happy sigh. "They treated me like part of the gang. Some of them were off on their own with husbands and wives. They'd all come and bring something to eat and share. I'd bring a big jar of pickles that they all loved so much. I might bring some beer. Those were happy days on Cambridge Street. And she let me be part of it."he added.

"So, Ronald asked me how it was going with Ellie one day at work. I said I was crazy about her. That my weekends with her family were great. That she would really only let me take her for walks. She didn't want to go anywhere that cost money. But, she had let me buy her a meatloaf dinner. I thought that was worth mentioning for some reason." he said.

"She let you buy her dinner? She let you pay for it?" roared Ronald. He clapped me on the back and said "You're doing great, Ralph. That girl never lets a guy buy her anything. She let you buy her meatloaf? Woo hooo!" he chuckled as he remembered that part.

"I don't know. She was skittish. She liked me a lot I could tell. But, I wasn't hurrying her. I didn't ask her to be my girlfriend or anything. I knew your mother wouldn't go for that. She didn't want anyone laying claim to her. I didn't have a lot of experience with girls but I could tell that. I just tried to make her happy." he explained.

"Meanwhile, her oldest brother Jimmy was speaking up for me. I didn't know it until a lot later. There were still a lot of young men swarming around Cambridge Street. She had just broken off writing to some soldier. Her brother Jimmy told her there were too many boys around. That people were going to start to talk. He told her it was time she picked one. He said I think you should go for the Swede. He is a hard worker. He loves his family. He loves you as much as I do. You can't do better than the Swede. I always liked that Jimmy." he said with a laugh.

"And then Christmas was coming. It got really cold out. We walked everywhere. She was never dressed warmly enough. If that girl had a warm coat? She probably made her little sister wear it. I was making enough money. I was saving. I couldn't go home to Maine for Christmas. It was too far. I mailed everyone little gifts. The rent on my room was all paid up. I even paid January's rent early. I knew my landlady could use the money for Christmas. She was a good soul. Always looking out for me. I hated seeing Ellie out on the streets not dressed warmly enough. It really bothered me. I would try to give her my coat and she would always say no." he said as he shook his head in wonder.

"Our walks at night took us by a department store. The windows were dressed up really pretty for Christmas. They were all twinkling lights and fake snow. We would always stop and look at the pretty windows. It was a nice store. It wasn't a fancy expensive place. It's where everyone shopped in the neighborhood. I bought my work clothes there. There was a beautiful ladies coat in the window. I noticed her looking at it every night. It was a pretty maroon color with a little fur like collar. I would go to open my mouth and say something when she was looking at that coat. She'd say "Don't. No!" and keep on walking."

"That went on for about two weeks. One night just before Christmas I spoke up when she was looking at that coat in the window. I couldn't stand it anymore. I said I haven't bought you a Christmas present yet. I am going to buy you a Christmas present. You don't need to buy me anything in return. I know you give your pay packet to your mother. Don't waste money on me. Give your brothers and sisters a good Christmas with your money. But, I am tired of you walking around and being so cold. I know you don't like it if a man spends money on you. But, I am going to buy you that coat. I don't expect anything in return. I am not trying to buy you by purchasing you a coat. I am going to buy you that coat because you are cold and I love you." he said in triumph.

"She looked me in the eye. She smiled at me so beautifully. She said to me............" he paused here to wipe his eyes with a paper napkin. He was hitting on the most important sentences anyone has ever said to him.

"She said to me 'If I let you buy me that coat? You do know what that means don't you? That means you are a man that is engaged to be married. Do you still want to buy me that coat?" he said. He was in awe remembering that moment.

"I just threw my head back and I howled at the moon! I grabbed her by the arm and dragged her into that store. The shop girl probably thought I was a little nuts. She couldn't get that coat off that mannequin fast enough for me. Dear, God! Hurry up woman before this girl changes her mind! I held that coat out for her. She put her arms in it. It fit her perfectly. She twirled around a few times to show me the coat from all sides. She was so happy. I'll never forget how happy she was. And, then? She kissed me and thanked me for the coat. She kissed me."

"I walked around with enough money to buy that coat in my wallet for weeks. I had put a big deposit on that coat. That's the only reason that beautiful coat was still on that mannequin in the window. Your mother never figured that one out thankfully." he said in hindsight.

"But, when she finally let me buy her that coat? That was the moment I knew she was mine." he ended his story.

****

And introducing: Mortimer; The Head Elf

A story where memoir meets fiction. Mortimer is a fictional character that has become very real to my family. He writes encouraging letters at Christmas time. He leaves packages full of arts and crafts to keep young people busy during that week before Christmas arrives. He deserves his own book. He'll get it soon. It's my promise to him and to all that love him. Except for Mortimer? The rest of the story is exactly as it happened.

Dedicated with much love to my parents.

Cardboard Box Christmas

Ralph was in trouble. His little girl Darlene was pretty angry with him. She had burst into tears and run to her room when she had discovered what he'd done. He hadn't meant to make her upset. He had just been cleaning and filling up his trash cans. He had no idea the box was so important.

Ralph was an engineer at Pratt and Whitney. He designed and tested jet engines. He loved his job even though he knew he worked too many hours. He spent every hour he had off either sleeping or making his family happy.

Ralph signed his little girl Darlene up for the Pratt and Whitney Children's Christmas Party. It was being held at the Bushnell Auditorium. It was a big company and they needed a big place for Santa to greet all the little children.

Ralph's older two children weren't interested anymore. His middle child had a paper route now. He couldn't sip apple cider and wait in line to see Santa anymore. He was too old for this part of Christmas.

His oldest boy was busy doing teenager things. But, Darlene believed in Santa. He enjoyed taking her to the company party. He was proud to show off his little girl to his work friends. His little girl. Looking just like her mother.

Ralph had held Darlene's hand tightly in the big crowd. They had sat in the auditorium while Mrs. Santa had led all the little children in a sing-a-long of Christmas carols. He had sung Jingle Bells at the top of his lungs right along with the children. Then it was time to stand in line to get a gift.

Girls stood in one line and boys in another. Santa had brought many helpers that day. Ralph recognized some of the secretaries from work dressed as elves. There were even a few of the managers up there wearing felt caps and pointy slippers. Everyone was in the spirit to make Christmas special for all the little children.

All the little girls that stood in line received a big box of doll dishes. Plastic plates, cups and saucers were lined up in rows. The box had little shelves to store the dishes. The bottom section of the box looked like a drawer. You pulled the little cardboard handle to find plastic silverware nestled inside.

Darlene was enchanted by the gift. She had enough Barbie dolls. Pratt and Whitney usually gave out Barbie dolls. This year Santa had exceeded her expectations.

Ralph tucked the box under his arm. He handed Darlene her bag of Christmas candy and held her hand to lead her across the street to the big parking lot. It had been a wonderful day between father and daughter.

Ralph looked around to see many men that he worked with holding on to their own little children. Every one was smiling. The men all glanced at each other and grinned. "This! This is what we work so hard for all year round!" they thought as they looked into the happy faces of their children.

Darlene got home and marched her new box of doll dishes out to her play house in the garage. The "dollhouse" held her extensive collection of dolls, doll furniture and play kitchen equipment. She set the box on the counter that Daddy had built her. She stood back to admire it and went in for dinner.

A few days later she bundled up against the cold. Darlene was in the mood to play "house". The garage was unheated but she played out there all year round.

Her parents both came running when they heard her wail.

Ralph and Ellie came into the small garage annex. They expected to see blood. The wail had been that loud. Instead they came face to face with a very angry little girl. The new plastic dishes that Santa had brought to the company party sat on the counter. They were in neat little rows. But, the box was gone.

The glorious box of cardboard. It had been sturdy. It had been constructed to hold those dishes forever. The designer had decorated it to look like a stenciled little dining room hutch.

It was gone.

Darlene pointed to the counter. Her face was bright red and the tears flowed down her face.

"Where is my box? The box is gone! The box was the best part! It was beautiful! It had shelves and a drawer. And, now it's gone!" she screamed. She kept staring at the space where she had put it. Perhaps it would reappear if she stared long enough.

Ellie looked at Ralph in confusion. She saw the look on his face and she said "Oh, no. You didn't." He nodded his head up and down at her. He had.

"I'm sorry, Little Girl. I didn't know. I was filling up my trash cans yesterday. I was gathering all the trash together. I was throwing out lots of boxes. I thought the important part was the dishes. I didn't think the box was special. I'm sorry. It's gone. The trash man picked it up yesterday." Daddy Ralph explained.

Darlene stared at him in disbelief. She pushed past him and went into the little house. She slammed the kitchen door behind her loudly. She didn't lock it. She knew her Mommy and Daddy were not dressed for the weather out there. She went into the bedroom and slammed the door. She was that angry.

Mommy Ellie heard the slamming of doors. She looked at her husband as he paced around the little doll house room. "Ralph. It was a cardboard box. How were you to know? Maybe you should ask before you throw things out. But, it was an honest mistake. She'll calm down. You're her Daddy. She can't stay angry at you for long."

Daddy Ralph stopped pacing. "That's the first time. She's never been angry at me before. Did you see her face? She couldn't even look at me. It was a box, Ellie! A cardboard box! And, now she's in there crying her eyes out over a box! " he said in disbelief.

"Oh, Ralph. That wasn't just any box. I can tell that was elf made. But, still. It was a mistake. Let it go." Ellie said as she drew him into the house.

They both stood in the warm little kitchen and listened. There was no crying coming from the closed bedroom.

Mommy Ellie knew that was a bad sign. An angry crying female will get over it quickly. An angry female that is quiet and staring at a wall is an all together scarier thing.

Ralph went to work the next day. Darlene had given him a kiss goodbye as usual. But, she hadn't asked him over and over if he had his thermos and his lunch box like she usually did. He had just received a quiet kiss on the cheek.

Ralph talked about it with the other engineers during their lunch hour. He described the scene when his little girl had discovered the box was missing. Three other men raised their hands. They had done the same thing. They had received their share of little girl wrath. One man said it was his first time ever without a little girl kiss goodnight.

Another described his whole day before getting to work for the second shift. He had gone from department store to department store. There were no more doll dish sets. Pratt and Whitney had bought them all so that every little girl could receive the same item. One manager of a toy department had even called the toy company for him. There were no more to be had.

"That was one well engineered box." one engineer was heard to whisper. They all finished their sandwiches in silence.

Ralph got home from work very late at night. He wrote a letter to his friend Mortimer. He described the situation. He asked for his help. He put a stamp on the envelope after writing Mortimer, North Pole on the front. He didn't even feel silly. Mortimer was a personal friend after all. Sometimes you just have to ask your friend the elf for help.

Ralph couldn't stand his little girl being angry at him. Darlene pretended everything was just as usual. But, he could feel it. She wasn't over it.

For the first time Ralph understood how wounding it could be to say "I'm disappointed in you." to one of his children. He vowed to never say that again. Darlene hadn't used those words. But, he felt them.

Mortimer was Santa's Head Elf. He visited on Columbus Street every year on the Saturday before Christmas. He caught up with one of his favorite families while eating copious amounts of bacon.

Mortimer was as chatty as ever the next Saturday. He was joyful and engaging. He told great North Pole jokes. But, he felt that something was off this year.

He nodded his pointy ears at Darlene. "What's with this one? She still believes or she wouldn't be sitting here eating my bacon. Is she just getting over being sick? Her joy is off." he said to Mommy Ellie.

Daddy Ralph answered instead. "Did you get my letter, Mortimer? I discussed this all in my letter. If you didn't get it? Don't worry about it. I'll figure something out."

"Ah! Yes, indeedy! Letters from this family are expressed to my desk. Still thinking on that one, Ralph. A tricky little problem. We'll discuss that on my way out if you will?" Mortimer said as he gave Ralph a 'be quiet' wink.

Mortimer made small talk. "So! I explained to the last family that this was my last visit there. Their little boy is on the brink of not believing. You all know as soon as I walk out the door you start to forget our visit. That's the way it's supposed to be. You can't be thinking about the North Pole all year. It isn't your domain. But, you know in flashes that I'm real. That Santa is real. That wishes and prayers are real. But, this little boy? Wouldn't even share his bacon with me." Mortimer said in a huff.

"You'll stop visiting if I stop believing?" asked Darlene. She was a little worried. She loved Christmas and she loved Mortimer. But, every year it got harder. All the kids at school no longer believed. She found herself being quiet when such things were discussed. She felt like a traitor not standing up for Mortimer. But, she didn't have time for the meanness of kids her age. And, boy they could be mean.

"You'll probably stop believing." said Mortimer. "You'll find your belief again some day. But, not until you have little children of your own. But, I'll never stop coming to this little house on Columbus Street. And, you know why?

"No, why?" asked Darlene.

"Because, of this one right here." he said as he pointed to Mommy Ellie. "She has never stopped believing. Her letters are received every single month of the year. There is no one that believes more than Ellie." He beamed at Mommy Ellie.

Ellie looked surprised. "It's true that I believe. But, letters? I haven't written a letter to Santa since 1935!" she exclaimed.

"Ellie! You write a letter every month! You send a letter to St. Anne's Shrine with a donation each and every month. You write out a list of names. Your dearly departed. You ask for prayers for their souls. You write the names of the sick. You write down your worries. Santa is a saint after all. He gets a copy. And your letters are always expressed to my desk as I mentioned before. Letter to Santa. Letter to a shrine? All one and the same, dear Ellie." explained Mortimer. "I'll never stop visiting you."

Ellie blushed at the attention she was receiving from the pointy eared Elf.

Mortimer jumped off his chair made taller by two big phone books.

"I'm off! Best breakfast I've had this hour! Goodbye until next year, ladies." he said as he bowed and waved his feathered cap at the females in the room. "If I could have a word at the door, Ralph?"

Ralph showed Mortimer to the front door that was saved for important company.

"Your letter, Ralph. That box that you threw out? Indeed Elf made. Don't feel bad. We all make mistakes. I can feel in the air that you're paying for this mistake. Darlene will get over it. I don't know that I can get a box to you in time for Christmas. The cardboard factory was done with those boxes in July. The machinery has been switched over to making Kissy Doll boxes for months now. I'll search but I don't think what you want exists right now. Don't you worry. The excitement of Christmas will make your little girl forget all about it. She's still got some belief inside of her." Mortimer explained quietly at the door.

Ralph looked disappointed but he squared his shoulders. He shook hands with the Head Elf.

"Well, it's good to know that you got the letter and that you tried. I can't ask for more than that. A very Merry Christmas to you Mortimer. Good to see you, as always." Ralph said as Mortimer disappeared into the sparkling brightness of the snow.

Ralph got to work in his own workshop.

Ellie kept Darlene out of the basement.

Mortimer got back to the North Pole and put out feelers. He was looking for a box of doll dishes. He told his search team that he didn't need the dishes. Just the box. They came back empty handed. Pratt and Whitney had taken them all.

Elves get two emergency wishes a year. Elves hardly ever use them. Especially, not for themselves. Many Elf wishes went unwished. Mortimer reached his arm towards the ceiling. He uttered an ancient Elf chant. He lowered his hand and pointed to the floor. When he opened his eyes a well constructed, super engineered empty cardboard box sat at his feet.

Ralph never asked for anything. He had asked this year. Mortimer felt fulfilled to give away one of his wishes to help such a man. He wrapped the gift himself in shiny red paper with little white snowmen. He handed the gift off to an assistant.

Mortimer felt a little dizzy because one of his wishes had been spent. A few Eggnogs should take that feeling away. Mortimer got out the cream and the eggs and the rum with a smile. He searched through his shelves for the nutmeg.

Christmas morning arrived. The air snapped with cold in Manchester, Ct. The little fireplace in the Columbus Street living room glowed with the warmth of a wood fire.

The Christmas tree blinked in the corner. The manger scene was complete all the way down to the little baby Jesus in his creche. The miniature elves skiied down the slopes in the scene under the tree.

The little living room was bursting with gifts for the family of five. Three children that usually liked to sleep in came awake early with a start. It was Christmas morning!

The older boys started gathering the Christmas stockings up to be opened. Darlene went into her parent's bedroom to wake them up. She wondered why they always looked so exhausted on Christmas morning. They always woke up like they had only been sleeping for a few hours. It was a mystery.

Mommy Ellie and Daddy Ralph stumbled into the living room. The noise coming out of their three children soon woke them up.

The presents in the corner were stacked pretty high. One of the boys played "Santa" and started to put the gifts into piles for each of them.

That's when Darlene saw the beautiful wooden cabinet leaning against the wall. The dainty miniature dish hutch stood near the Christmas tree. It was made of real wood. The wood was the color of honey. The wooden chest had three drawers and two shelves. The shelves had a groove in them to hold up dishes.

Darlene felt the wood. It was warm from the glow of the fireplace. She smelled the varnish that made the piece of furniture shiny. She knelt down in front of it. She noticed the hearts stenciled in red paint across the drawers. She opened each one and sniffed the odor of newly cut wood. She ran her hands across the shelves and pictured her doll dishes displayed in splendor.

"What do you think, Little Girl? That's a nice china hutch for your doll dishes. Santa did good, didn't he?" asked Daddy from right behind her.

There was no tag on the little piece of handmade furniture. No where did it say "To Darlene; from Santa."

"Oh, Daddy! It's so beautiful! It's perfect! This will fit just right in the corner of my doll house. But, Daddy! This isn't from Santa! You made this for me. You even painted little red hearts on it. It's my favorite Christmas present ever! Thank you!" said Darlene as she threw her arms around her Daddy.

Darlene noticed the red paint under Daddy's fingernails at that very minute. She knew she was right though Daddy never said "You're welcome." He pretended that Santa had built that cupboard.

One of the last gifts lingered under the tree. It was large and square but lightweight. The tag said To Ralph; from Mortimer. It was wrapped in beautiful shiny red paper with little white snowmen on it. Ellie looked at Ralph with a question in her eyes. He shrugged his shoulders.

Darlene handed the present to Daddy. They all watched the last gift being unwrapped. Ralph tore the paper off and looked at the gift in astonishment. It was a well constructed, super engineered empty box. It was designed to hold doll dishes.

He put his head back and laughed. "Well, look at that! " he exclaimed.

Daddy handed the box to Darlene. "Here you go, Little Girl. This is to replace the box that I threw out. I'll never do that again without asking you first. I'm sorry you got so upset." he said.

Darlene looked confused. She got up and went over to her new wooden chest of drawers. She traced a heart with her finger.

"Whatever will I do with that, Daddy? What do I want with a cardboard box when I have this?" she asked in confusion. She handed the box back to him.

"Well! I know what we can do with this box. I have a friend at work that spent a whole day going from store to store looking for a box like this. He wanted it for his little girl. I'll give this to him tomorrow. It will make him very happy to have this." he said as he set the box aside.

Darlene said that sounded like a fine idea to her.

At the North Pole Mortimer felt his wish come back to him. He put out his hands and bounced on the balls of his feet. He felt even again. The feeling of being slightly off kilter disappeared. Ralph hadn't needed that box after all.

But, the eggnog had taken affect. Mortimer had no need of two wishes that would expire on New Years Eve. He picked up a snow globe that sat on the table next to his recliner. He shook it as he chanted. He envisioned a little white Cape Cod house at the bottom of Columbus Street in Manchester, Connecticut, USA.

He shook the snow globe.

Ralph stepped over his children playing with their new toys on the living room floor. His beautiful Ellie was cooking the bacon and scrambling the eggs. He sighed in contentment as he watched big fat snow flakes start to come down outside his picture window.

"Merry Christmas Mortimer, my dear old friend." Ralph said quietly as he watched the snow cover Columbus Street.

Merry Christmas to you and yours!